# AIRCRAFT
# A/R/C/H/I/V/E

## CLASSICS OF WORLD WAR TWO

Argus Books
Wolsey House
Wolsey Road
Hemel Hempstead
Herts. HP2 4SS
England

First published by Argus Books 1989

© In this Collection Argus Books 1989

ISBN 0 85242 985 1

Designed by Little Oak Studios
Phototypesetting by Typesetters (Birmingham) Ltd
Printed and bound in Great Britain by
William Clowes Limited, Beccles and London

Services and
sport of Henstridge,
gain over Southern

# AIRCRAFT ARCHIVE

## CLASSICS OF WORLD WAR TWO

# Contents

*A DETAILED COLLECTION OF ORIGINAL SCALE AIRCRAFT DRAWINGS*

# Introduction

In this, the seventh in our series of volumes on aircraft of World War II, we cover those types which do not necessarily fall neatly into the category of fighter or bomber, or which might otherwise be regarded as 'classics' of design or achievement. They include trainers, reconnaissance aircraft, communications aircraft, fleet spotters, a couple of noteworthy 'one-offs', and famous fighters which became national symbols characterised by shape and valiant battle records in the defence of their country.

Every aviation enthusiast has a personal favourite, and this selection of eighteen drawings must surely embrace more than a few of those first-loves. Many a pilot has good cause to express affection for the first primary trainer on which the treasured 'wings' were won. So we have the De Havilland 82A Tiger Moth, which provided the backbone of Elementary Flying Training Schools in the UK, the Union of South Africa, Rhodesia and Australia, and the Boeing-Stearman Kaydet which did such yeoman service in the Airschools of Canada and the USA. One stage on, and the Bücker Bü 133 Jungmeister is on record as the finest mount for solo aerobatics of its time, while for long and amazingly varied application the Polikarpov Po-2 must be included as the most adaptable workhorse ever to carry Soviet stars.

◀ The remarkable Fi 156 Storch was designed in 1935 and became a true workhorse of WWII. French-built Storchs are still flying, more than fifty years later. (IWM B7394)

For 'macho' shape, those monoplane fighters with open cockpits, the I-16 Rata and Macchi C200 Saetta, lend comparison with the heroic Polish PZL P-11c and the first (and last) of the German biplane fighters, the Heinkel He 51. Who can ignore those candidates for being slowest, the Storch and Lysander? Differing approaches to the same specification with similar achievement provide the aero-enthusiast with inspiration to model those daredevil tools of subterfuge.

One could go on – the elegant form of the Stösser, the last-ever biplane project in the Canadian Gregor and the encapsulated power of the Martin-Baker MB5 all demand study. But one aircraft stands above all, and for that reason, we allocate more space to the Focke-Wulf Fw 190. Drawn impeccably by Arthur Bentley to the most finite detail, this set of drawings represents the epitome of type-study and patient interpretation of remaining references as well as actual aircraft.

As we have mentioned in other volumes, every one of these drawings is a tribute to the skill and dedication of amateur researchers who produce something which very few of the manufacturers can provide! One such example is the Tiger Moth. Another which we dare claim as

◀ The preserved Macchi C200 on display at the Vigna di Valle Air Force Museum near Rome. Detailed plans of this famous fighter can be found on pages 60–64.

being more correct than any previous plan is that for the Polikarpov I-16, a drawing which we are publishing for the first time in these pages. BUT – knowing how fastidious many of our aeronautical 'nuts' are, we quite expect to be told that a line is a half millimetre or so out of place before the ink has a chance to dry! Another aspect with which we are specially pleased is that for the eighteen drawings we have sixteen different draughtsmen whose work has appeared over the years in the pages of *Aeromodeller* and *Scale Models*, and it is with universal gratitude, from ourselves as publishers and from the readers as consumers, that we acknowledge the contribution made by Arthur Bentley, Maurice Brett, Dennis Bryant, George Cox, Tony Datkiewicz, Geoff Duval, Bert Hatton, Björn Karlström, Pat Lloyd, Bill Nicholls, Felix Pawlowicz, Dave Platt, Giuliani Raimondi, Harry Robinson, Ian Stair and Harry Woodman to the annals of aviation history.

A *Jagdfliegerschule* prewar, showing Fw 56s (left), He 51s (right foreground) and Ar 65s in a mixture of *Luftwaffe* and civil markings; the Heinkel and Focke Wulf aircraft are featured in this volume.
▼

# Polikarpov Po-2

**Country of origin:** USSR.
**Type:** Two-seat, land based training and general-purpose aircraft.
**Dimensions:** Wing span 37ft 4in *11.38m*; length 26ft 1in *7.95m*.

**Weights:** Empty 1918lb *870kg*.
**Powerplant:** One M-11 radial engine rated at 100hp.
**Performance:** Maximum speed 93mph *150kph*; service ceiling 12,530ft *3820m*;

range 250 miles *400km*.
**Armament:** None as trainer; various light ordnance when used in offensive roles.
**Service:** First flight 1927.

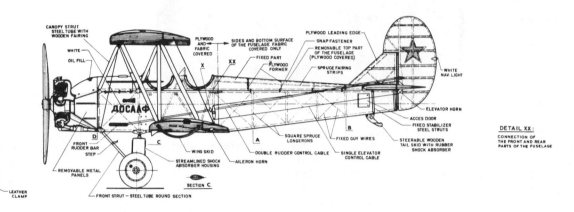

▲ Port elevation, Standard aircraft

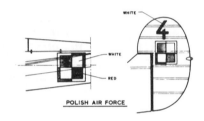

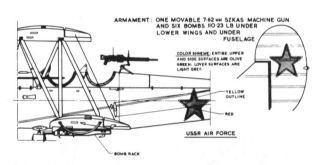

◄ Scrap port elevation, Army version

Polish Po-2 (CSS-13) in Army service. Licence-built Polish machines featured tubular struts, revised control surfaces and undercarriage, and other modifications. (M Passingham)
▼

▲
Soviet Po-2 serving as a liaison and communications aircraft. The Po-2's flying surfaces were fabric covered, as were the sides and bottom of the fuselage. (M Passingham)

**Scale**

0 1 2 3 4 5 6 7 8 ft
0           1           2 m

▲
**Fuselage cross-sections**

SECTION E

**Wing cross-section ▲**
*Upper and lower wing*

TOP AND LOWER WING OF SIMILAR TWO-SPAR
ALL WOOD STRUCTURE. OPTIONAL AUXILIARY
PETROL TANK IN WING CENTER SECTION
19·5 GAL. CAPACITY.

PLYWOOD LEADING EDGE
FIXED GUY WIRES
RED STAR
FALSE SPAR
COMPRESSION RIB
SPRUCE FRONT SPAR
WING RIB
RED NAV. LIGHT
YELLOW OUTLINE
STAGGER 2·62'
E

HAND HOLD
AILERON HORN
SPRUCE REAR SPAR
AILERONS GAP WIRES
STREAMLINED SECTION
SPRUCE STRIP
WING ATTACHMENT FITTING
WING WALK REINFORCEMENT WITH STEPS
1" WIDE PINKED RIB TAPE
SIGHTING SLIT (ARMY VERSION ONLY) ON THE RIGHT LOWER WING
WOODEN FAIR-LEAD
ELEVATOR HORN

▲
**Plan view, Standard aircraft**

METAL WHEEL DISC
TURNBUCKLE
STREAMLINED AXLE HOUSING
STRANDED STEEL BRACING WIRES
TIRE VALVE ACCESS HOLE

▲
**Scrap view**
*Undercarriage details*

◄ Two members of the Soviet 46th 'Tamanskii' Guards Light Night Bomber Regiment, a unit whose personnel were exclusively female, pose in front of their Po-2s. (W Klepacki)

Ambulance version, showing method of transporting stretcher cases. Note external control wires running along fuselage. (M Passingham) ►

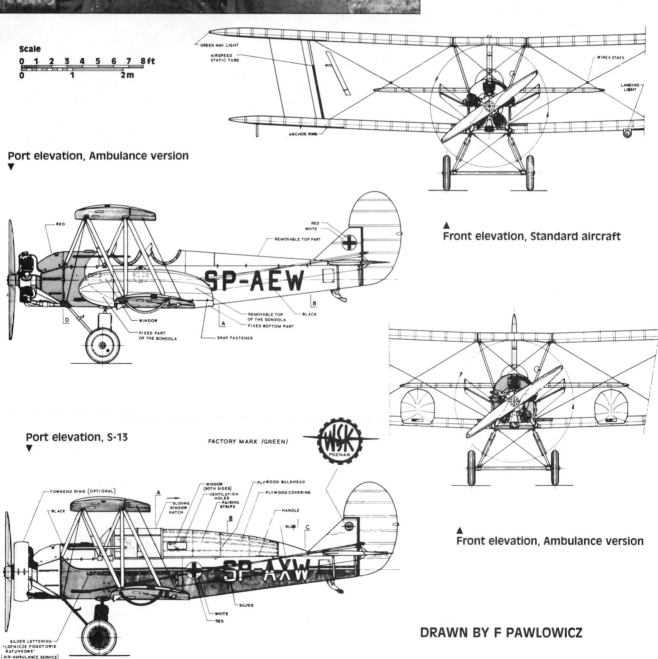

**Scale**

0 1 2 3 4 5 6 7 8 ft

0       1       2m

GREEN NAV. LIGHT

AIRSPEED STATIC TUBE

WIRES STAYS

LANDING LIGHT

ANCHOR RING

**Port elevation, Ambulance version**
▼

RED

RED WHITE

REMOVABLE TOP PART

**SP-AEW**

WINDOW

FIXED PART OF THE GONDOLA

REMOVABLE TOP OF THE GONDOLA

FIXED BOTTOM PART

SNAP FASTENER

BLACK

▲
**Front elevation, Standard aircraft**

**Port elevation, S-13**
▼

FACTORY MARK /GREEN/

WSK POZNAŃ

TOWNEND RING (OPTIONAL)

BLACK

WINDOW (BOTH SIDES)

VENTILATION HOLES

SLIDING WINDOW HATCH

FAIRING STRIPS

PLYWOOD BULKHEAD

PLYWOOD COVERING

HANDLE

BLUE

**SP-AXW**

LOTNICZE

SILVER

WHITE
RED

SILVER LETTERING "LOTNICZE POGOTOWIE RATUNKOWE" (AIR-AMBULANCE SERVICE)

▲
**Front elevation, Ambulance version**

**DRAWN BY F PAWLOWICZ**

## Colour notes

**Ambulance version:** Entire fuselage, wings, tail, undercarriage and gondolas – light cream.

**S-13:** All surfaces of wings and tail, all wing struts – silver. Front, lower sides and undersurfaces of fuselage, undercarriage – blue.

**Standard aircraft:** All surfaces of wings and tail, fuselage, all struts and undercarriage – olive green. Propeller – black or varnish.

**Army version:** Entire upper and side surfaces – olive green. Lower surfaces – light grey.

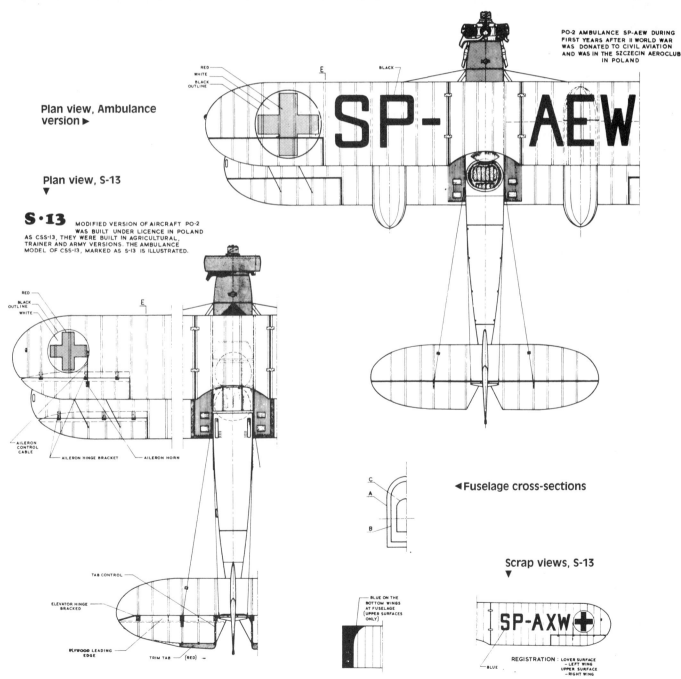

PO-2 AMBULANCE SP-AEW DURING FIRST YEARS AFTER II WORLD WAR WAS DONATED TO CIVIL AVIATION AND WAS IN THE SZCZECIN AEROCLUB IN POLAND

**Plan view, Ambulance version ▶**

RED
WHITE
BLACK OUTLINE

E

BLACK

# SP- AEW

**Plan view, S-13 ▼**

## S·13
MODIFIED VERSION OF AIRCRAFT PO-2 WAS BUILT UNDER LICENCE IN POLAND AS CSS-13, THEY WERE BUILT IN AGRICULTURAL, TRAINER AND ARMY VERSIONS. THE AMBULANCE MODEL OF CSS-13, MARKED AS S-13 IS ILLUSTRATED.

RED
BLACK OUTLINE
WHITE

E

AILERON CONTROL CABLE

AILERON HINGE BRACKET     AILERON HORN

TAB CONTROL

ELEVATOR HINGE BRACKED

PLYWOOD LEADING EDGE

TRIM TAB (RED)

C
A
B

**◀Fuselage cross-sections**

BLUE ON THE BOTTOM WINGS AT FUSELAGE (UPPER SURFACES ONLY)

BLUE

**Scrap views, S-13 ▼**

## SP-AXW✚

REGISTRATION : LOWER SURFACE – LEFT WING
UPPER SURFACE – RIGHT WING

BLUE

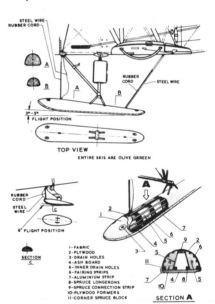

Polikarpov U-2 trainers, the furthest aircraft bearing a civil registration although a similar-style tail number to the other. (M Passingham) ▲

Polish-built CSS-13 equipped with ski undercarriage. Note also landing light beneath port wing, and wing-tip skids. (M Passingham) ▼

**Scrap view (not to scale)**
*Instrument panel (front cockpit), S-13/CSS-13*
▼

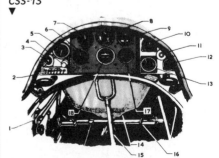

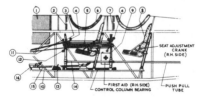

**Scrap view, Standard aircraft**
*Cockpit details* ▲

**Key to instrument panel**
1. Throttle. 2. Electrical control. 3. Ignition switch. 4. Pneumatic fuel gauge. 5. Fuel gauge switch. 6. Airspeed indicator. 7. Altimeter. 8. Compass. 9. Turn and bank indicator. 10. Tachometer. 11. Engine primer. 12. Carburettor air thermometer. 13. Engine gauge. 14. Fuel tank (33.5gal capacity). 15. Control stick. 16. Rudder bar. 17. Rate of climb indicator. 18. Artificial horizon.

**Key to cockpit details**
1. Fuel tank. 2. Front instrument panel. 3. Pilot's control stick. 4. Throttle lever. 5. Wood bracket (port side). 6. Padded lining. 7. Rear instrument panel. 8. Seat. 9. Rear control stick (detachable). 10. Floorboard. 11. Mixture control lever. 12. Engine heater shut off. 13. Starting magneto (starboard side). 14. Control column thrust tube. 15. Rudder bar thrust tube. 16. Main rudder bar.

# De Havilland DH82A Tiger Moth

**Country of origin:** Great Britain.
**Type:** Two-seat, land-based primary trainer.
**Dimensions:** Wing span 29ft 4in *8.94m*; length 23ft 11in *7.29m*; height 8ft 9½in *2.68m*; wing area 239 sq ft *22.2m²*.
**Weights:** Empty 1115lb *506kg*; maximum 1825lb *828kg*.
**Powerplant:** One De Havilland Gipsy Major four-cylinder, inverted, air-cooled engine rated at 130hp.
**Performance:** Maximum speed 109mph *175kph* at sea level; initial climb rate 673ft/min *196m/min*; service ceiling 13,600ft *4150m*.
**Armament:** None.
**Service:** First flight (DH60T) September 1931, (prototype Tiger Moth) 26 October 1931; service entry November 1931.

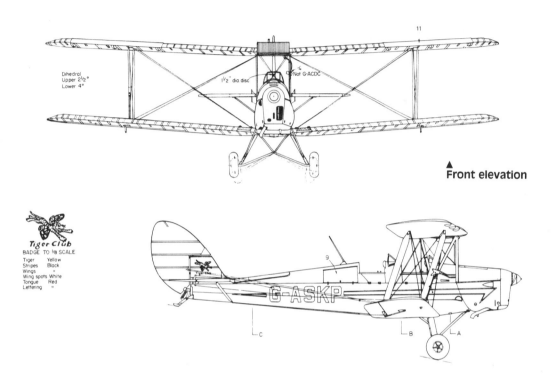

▲ Front elevation

Tiger Club
BADGE TO ⅛ SCALE
Tiger        Yellow
Stripes      Black
Wings        "
Wing spots   White
Tongue       Red
Lettering    "

▲ Starboard elevation

A Royal Navy Tiger Moth, photographed in 1947 at Eaton Bray. This aircraft was formerly G-ABRC, impressed into military service *circa* 1940.
▼

▲
**G-ADUK of the London Aeroplane Club, being flown solo, 1948. Nearly 9000 Tiger Moths were built, many being released to civil flying clubs postwar at knock-down prices. (De Havilland)**

**Scrap view**
*Instrument panel*
▼

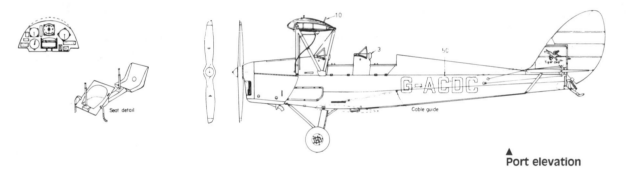

Seat detail

Cable guide

▲
Port elevation

**Tiger Moth II R5130 in wartime colours of Dark Earth and Dark Green camouflage, with yellow undersurfaces.**
▼

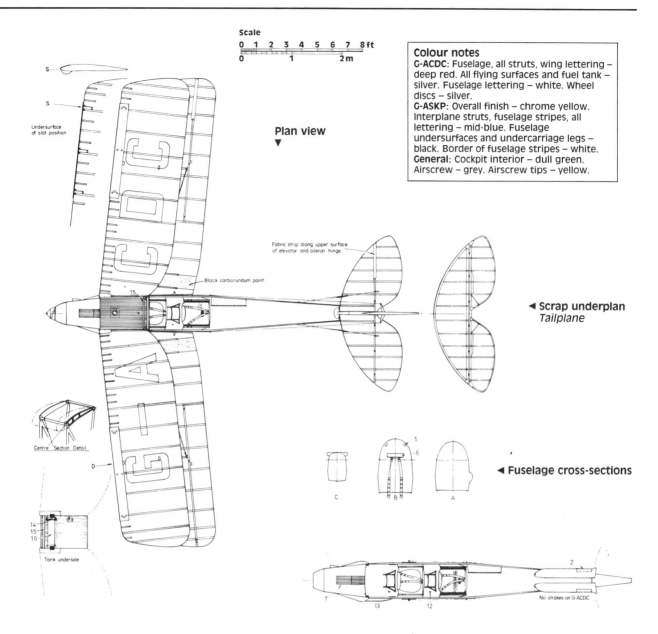

Scale

0 1 2 3 4 5 6 7 8 ft
0         1         2 m

S

Undersurface
of slot position

S

**Plan view**
▼

Fabric strip along upper surface
of elevator and aileron hinge

Black carborundum paint

15

◄ **Scrap underplan**
*Tailplane*

Centre Section Detail

D

14
15
16

Tank underside

◄ **Fuselage cross-sections**

5
6

C        B   A

No strokes on G-ACDC

7        13      12      2

▲
**Scrap plan view**
*Fuselage, with wing omitted*

**One of the 3000 or so Tiger Moths built by Morris Motors
during the war. Note the first aid access panel just aft of
the roundel.**
▼

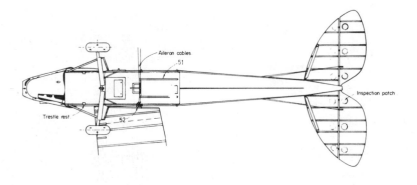

Aileron cables
51

Inspection patch

Trestle rest
52

**▲ Scrap underplan**

A flight of Tiger Moths, two in military markings, photographed prewar. During the desperate days of 1940, plans were laid to use the type as a fighter and a bomber should the need arise. (De Havilland) ▶

Scale

0 1 2 3 4 5 6 7 8 ft
0       1       2 m

**Scrap view**
*Structure*
▼

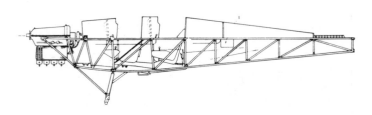

**Scrap views ▲**
*Fin and rudder construction*

**Scrap port elevation**
*Interplane struts*
▼

D

1½ dia. disc

8

F

Tie down eye
at base of strut

E

Cockpit instrumentation is basic, as befits a primary trainer. The crash pads are prominent in this view, which also shows to advantage the non-slip wing walk area for the crew.
▼

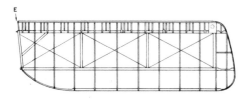

E

**▲ Scrap underplan**
*Upper port wing*

**Scrap underplan**
*Lower port wing*
▼

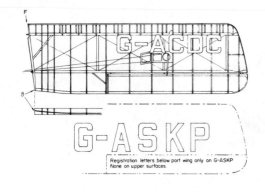

F

G-ACDC

8

G-ASKP

Registration letters below port wing only on G-ASKP
None on upper surfaces

**DRAWN BY D BRYANT**

## Numerical key

1. First aid stowage. 2. Chafing plates on anti-spin strakes. 3. Leather-covered crash pad. 4. Rear-view mirror. 5. Handgrips (front cockpit only). 6. Slot for safety harness. 7. Corrugated step plate. 8. Trailing edge slopes up from aileron to root. 9. Intercom and baggage stowage. 10. Fuel gauge. 11. Slots. 12. Magneto switches. 13. Oil tank (mounted externally for cooling). 14. Metal retaining plates. 15. Corrugations flattened locally to give smooth strip. 16. Flat cover plate over spar channel in tank. 17. Connector pipe across bridge of tank. 18. Fuel sump. 19. Fuel shut-off rod. 20. Drain cock. 21. Venturi (both sides). 22. Pressed aluminium fairing. 23. Overflow pipe fairing. 24. Steadying arm for aileron return cable. 25. Filler cap. 26. Overflow valve. 27. Skid detail. 28. Carburettor air intake. 29. Aileron cam detail. 30. Leather cuff. 31. Map pocket. 32. Spring bias on rudder. 33. Slot locking lever. 34. Slot locking handgrips. 35. Parallel-action rudder pedals. 36. Front seat mounted in diagonal bulkhead. 37. Jacking pad. 38. Rudder linking rod. 39. Spring bias for tail trimming. 40. Door catches. 41. Tail trim connecting rod. 42. Throttle. 43. Air speed indicator. 44. Deviation card holder. 45. Altimeter. 46. Crash pad. 47. Turn and bank indicator. 48. Engine speed indicator. 49. Oil pressure indicator (red). 50. Pull tab for first aid access. 51. ¾in × ½in wood strips. 52. Pitot tubes.

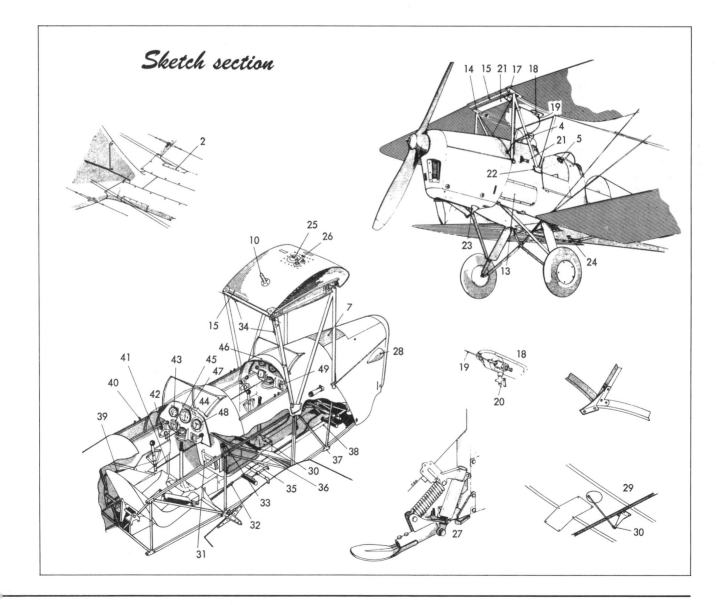

*Sketch section*

# PZL P11c

**Country of origin:** Poland.
**Type:** Single-seat, land-based interceptor fighter and fighter-bomber.
**Dimensions:** Wing span 35ft 2in *10.79m*; length 24ft 9½in *7.56m*; height 9ft 4in *2.84m*; wing area 192.7 sq ft *17.9m²*.
**Weights:** Empty 2443lb *1108kg*; loaded

3505lb *1590kg*.
**Powerplant:** One Bristol Mercury VI S2 nine-cylinder radial engine rated at 645hp.
**Performance:** Maximum speed 242mph *390kph* at 18,050ft *5500m*; time to 16,400ft *5000m*, 6min; service ceiling

36,100ft *11,000m*; range 503 miles *810km*.
**Armament:** Two or four fixed 7.7mm KM Wz33 machine guns, plus two 27lb *12.25kg* bombs.
**Service:** First flight (P11/I prototype) October 1931; service entry (P11a) 1934, (P11c) late 1934.

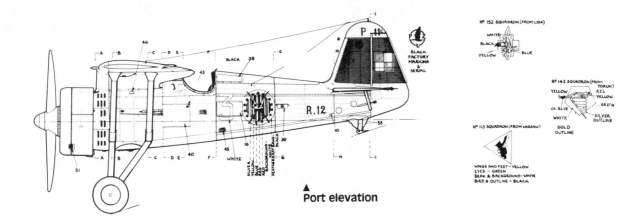

▲ Port elevation

**Colour notes**
Olive green overall except lower surfaces of wings and tailplane which were light blue-grey.

No 113 Squadron Polish Air Force P11cs at Okecie Airport, Warsaw; the fourth machine in line is in fact a P6, as noted on the fin tip. Emergency production of the P11 was halted by the German invasion, and only some 250 were built. (M Passingham)
▼

## Numerical key

1. Mirror. 2. Fuel tank. 3. Hand grip. 4. Compass. 5. Boost. 6. Fuel pressure. 7. Emergency fuel cut-off. 8. Oil temperature (out). 9. Brake drum and cable. 10. Jacking point. 11. Fuel gauge. 12. Oil temperature (in). 13. Oil pressure. 14. Air speed indicator/artificial horizon. 15. Compass deviation table. 16. Bank indicator. 17. Engine rpm. 18. Altimeter. 19. Rate of fuel flow control. 20. Clock. 21. Bomb release control. 22. Harness tension control. 23. Boost control. 24. Throttle. 25. Radio. 26. Fuselage guns trigger button. 27. Wing guns trigger button. 28. Oil tank. 29. Fuel header tank. 30. Rudder pedals. 31. Brake control. 32. Ammunition box. 33. Dual-purpose ailerons/flaps. 34. Signal cartridges rack. 35. Gun mountings. 36. Elevator trim. 37. Very pistol. 38. Pilot's locker. 39. First aid. 40. Gun servicing hatch. 41. Air intake control. 42. Seat adjustment. 43. Opening for Very pistol. 44. Elevator trim gear. 45. Foot rests. 46. Fuel inlet. 47. Bomb rack (12.5kg). 48. Air speed indicator pitot. 49. Venturi. 50. Oil cooler. 51. Exhaust. 52. Exhaust collector. 53. Corrugated duralumin (8 corrugations per inch). 54. Rubber covering (to prevent shell damage by cases and links). 55. Tan leather. 56. Detachable panel over oil tank. 57. KM Wz33 guns. 58. Camera.

▲ The PZL P6 prototype. This and the P7 were the direct progenitors of the P11, the inline-engined P8/9/10 series being discarded in favour of the radial-engined 7 and 11. (M Passingham)

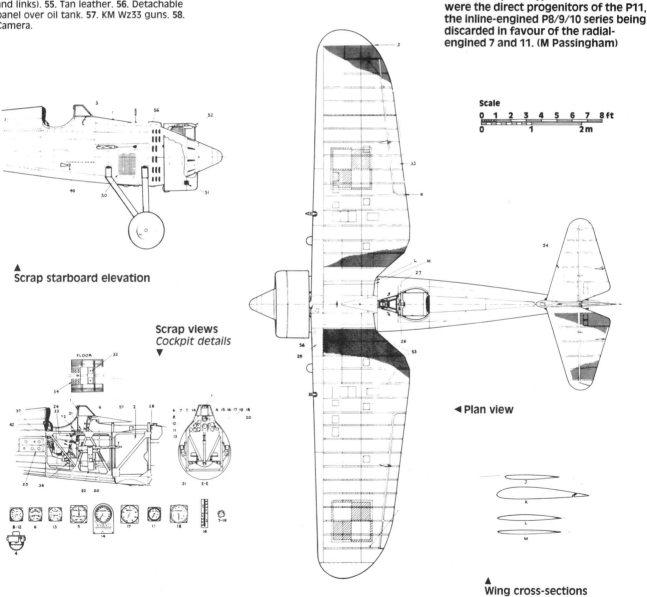

▲ Scrap starboard elevation

**Scrap views**
*Cockpit details*
▼

Scale
0 1 2 3 4 5 6 7 8 ft
0 1 2 m

◄ Plan view

▲ Wing cross-sections

## DRAWN BY Z A DATKIEWICZ

▲ A captured P11c is manhandled away. Note the faded national insignia on the upper wing and the 113 ('Owl') Squadron marking on the fuselage. (M Passingham)

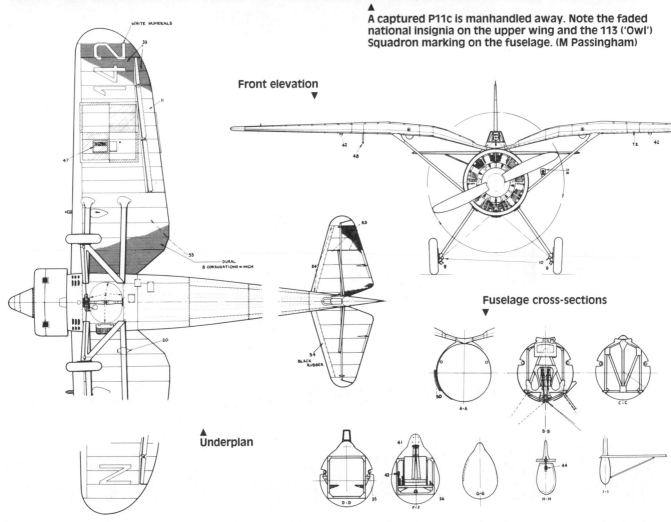

Front elevation ▼

Fuselage cross-sections ▼

▲ Underplan

# Heinkel He 51B-1

**Country of origin:** Germany.
**Type:** Single-seat, land-based fighter.
**Dimensions:** Wing span 36ft 1in *11.00m*; length 27ft 6¾in *8.40m*; height 10ft 6in *3.20m*; wing area 292.78 sq ft *27.2m²*.
**Weights:** Empty 3247lb *1472kg*; normal loaded 4189lb *1900kg*.

**Powerplant:** One BMW VI 7.3Z twelve-cylinder, liquid-cooled engine rated at 750hp.
**Performance:** Maximum speed 205mph *330kph* at sea level; time to 3280ft *1000m*, 1.4min; service ceiling 25,260ft *7700m*; range 354 miles *570km*.

**Armament:** Two fixed 7.9mm MG 17 machine guns.
**Service:** First flight (He 51a) summer 1933, (He 51A-0) July 1934, (A-1) April 1935; service entry (B-1) early 1936.

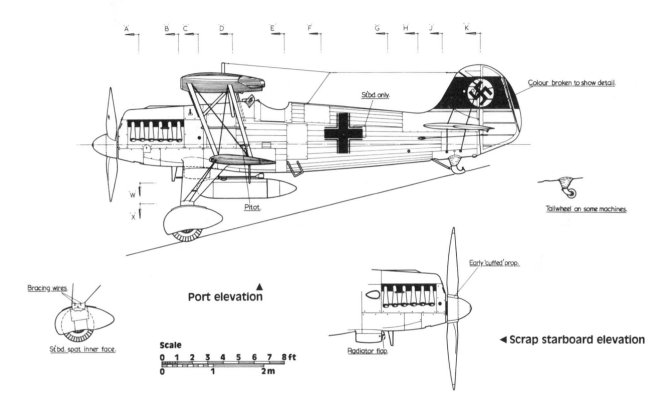

Colour broken to show detail.

Stbd. only.

Tailwheel on some machines.

Pitot.

W
X

Bracing wires.

Stbd. spat inner face.

**Port elevation**

**Scale**
0 1 2 3 4 5 6 7 8 ft
0 1 2m

Early 'cuffed' prop.

Radiator flap.

◄ **Scrap starboard elevation**

He 51A, probably the first A-0 pre-production aircraft D-IQEE. Differences between the A and B versions were minimal. (M Passingham)

**DRAWN BY C J NICHOLLS**

A 1934 photograph showing three pre-production He 51s; A-05 (nearest camera) and A-04 can be identified. (Pilot Press)

**Notes**
**He 51A-1:** Single undercarriage bracing; cuffed propeller.
**He 51B-1:** Double undercarriage bracing; external fuel tank. All types sometimes discarded spats.

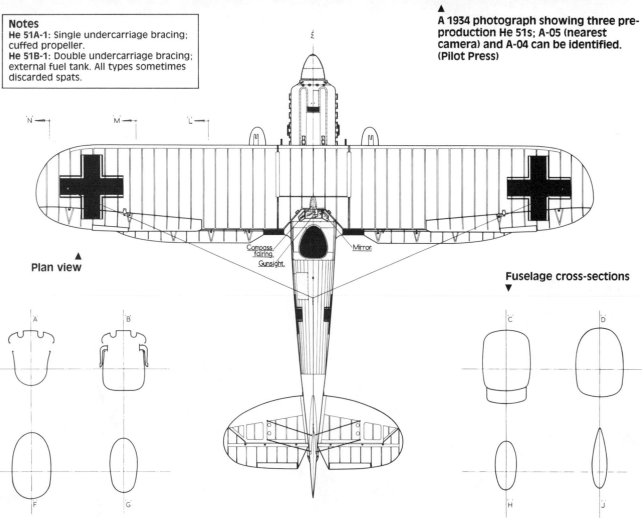

▲
**Plan view**

Compass fairing.
Gunsight.
Mirror.

**Fuselage cross-sections**
▼

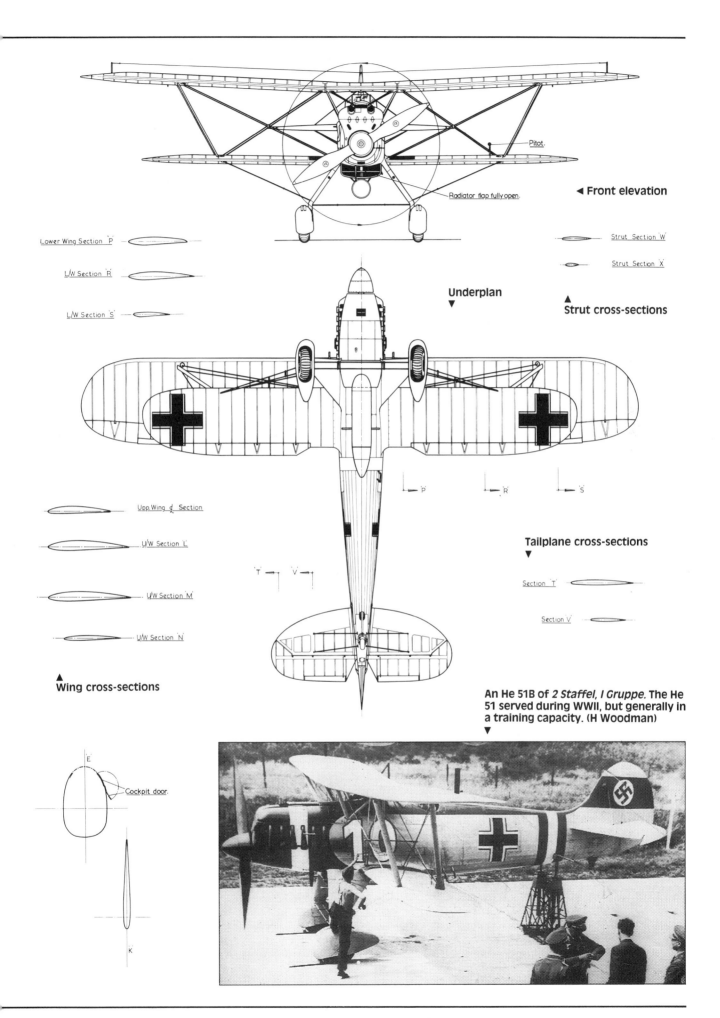

◄ **Front elevation**

Radiator flap fully open.

Pitot.

Lower Wing Section 'P'

L/W Section 'R'

L/W Section 'S'

Strut Section 'W'

Strut Section 'X'

**Underplan**
▼

▲
**Strut cross-sections**

Upp.Wing d Section

U/W Section 'L'

U/W Section 'M'

U/W Section 'N'

▲
**Wing cross-sections**

'P'   'R'   'S'

**Tailplane cross-sections**
▼

Section 'T'

Section 'V'

'T'   'V'

An He 51B of *2 Staffel, I Gruppe*. The He 51 served during WWII, but generally in a training capacity. (H Woodman)
▼

E

Cockpit door.

K

# Focke-Wulf Fw 56 Stösser (Falcon)

**Country of origin:** Germany.
**Type:** Single-seat, land-based advanced trainer.
**Dimensions:** Wing span 34ft 7½in *10.55m*; length 25ft 1in *7.65m*; height 8ft 4½in *2.55m*; wing area 150.7 sq ft *14.0m²*.
**Weights:** Empty 1477lb *670kg*; loaded

2172lb *985kg*.
**Powerplant:** One Argus As 10C eight-cylinder, inverted-vee, air-cooled engine rated at 240hp.
**Performance:** Maximum speed 173mph *278kph* at sea level; time to 3280ft *1000m*, 2.2min; service ceiling 20,340ft

6200m; range 239 miles *385km*.
**Armament:** One or two fixed 7.92mm MG 17 machine guns, plus up to three 22lb *10kg* bombs.
**Service:** First flight (Fw 56 V1) November 1933; service entry 1937.

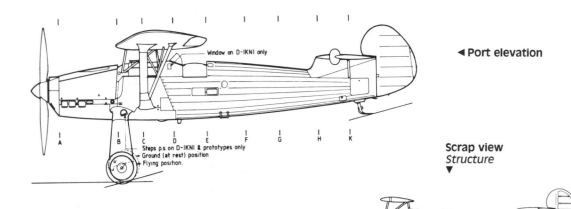

◄ **Port elevation**

Window on D-IKNI only

Steps p.s. on D-IKNI & prototypes only
Ground (at rest) position
Flying position.

**Scrap view**
*Structure*
▼

**Fuselage cross-sections**
▼

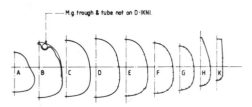

M.g. trough & tube not on D-IKNI.

Head-on shot of D-IIZE shows the elegant streamlining of the Fw 56 parasol fighter-trainer. The asymmetric exhaust pipes are well in evidence here.
▼

The celebrated aerobatic pilot Gerd Achgelis poses in his non-standard Stösser demonstrator D-IKNI (270hp Argus) at Los Angeles before the war. ►

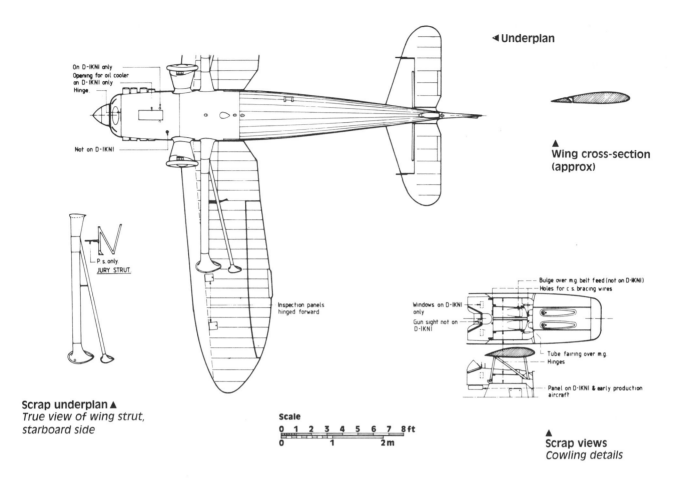

◀ Underplan

On D-IKNI only
Opening for oil cooler
on D-IKNI only
Hinge

Not on D-IKNI

P.s only.
JURY STRUT.

Inspection panels
hinged forward

**Wing cross-section
(approx)** ▲

Bulge over m.g. belt feed (not on D-IKNI)
Holes for c.s. bracing wires

Windows on D-IKNI
only

Gun sight not on
D-IKNI

Tube fairing over m.g.
Hinges

Panel on D-IKNI & early production
aircraft

**Scrap underplan** ▲
*True view of wing strut,
starboard side*

Scale

| 0 | 1 | 2 | 3 | 4 | 5 | 6 | 7 | 8 ft |

| 0 | 1 | 2m |

▲
**Scrap views**
*Cowling details*

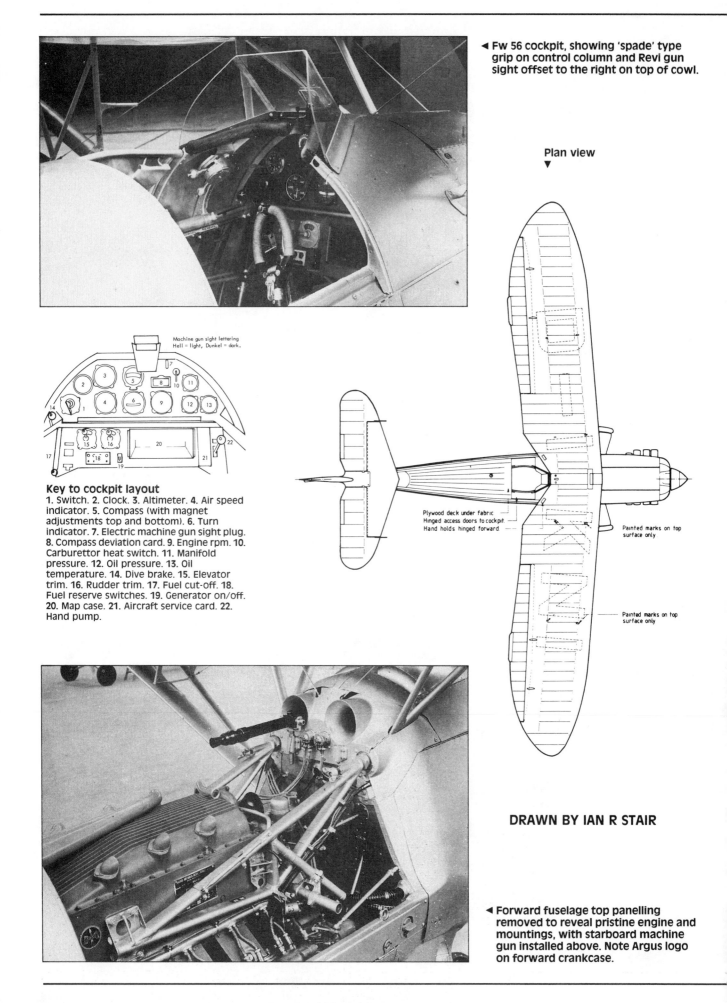

◄ Fw 56 cockpit, showing 'spade' type grip on control column and Revi gun sight offset to the right on top of cowl.

Plan view
▼

Machine gun sight lettering
Hell = light, Dunkel = dark.

### Key to cockpit layout
1. Switch. 2. Clock. 3. Altimeter. 4. Air speed indicator. 5. Compass (with magnet adjustments top and bottom). 6. Turn indicator. 7. Electric machine gun sight plug. 8. Compass deviation card. 9. Engine rpm. 10. Carburettor heat switch. 11. Manifold pressure. 12. Oil pressure. 13. Oil temperature. 14. Dive brake. 15. Elevator trim. 16. Rudder trim. 17. Fuel cut-off. 18. Fuel reserve switches. 19. Generator on/off. 20. Map case. 21. Aircraft service card. 22. Hand pump.

Plywood deck under fabric
Hinged access doors to cockpit
Hand holds hinged forward

Painted marks on top surface only

Painted marks on top surface only

**DRAWN BY IAN R STAIR**

◄ Forward fuselage top panelling removed to reveal pristine engine and mountings, with starboard machine gun installed above. Note Argus logo on forward crankcase.

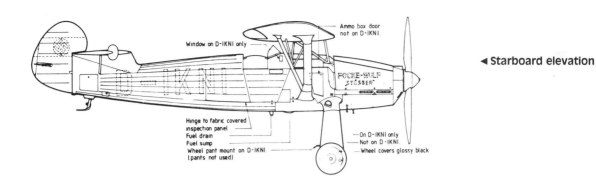

◄ Starboard elevation

Ammo box door not on D-IKNI.

Window on D-IKNI only

FOCKE-WULF "STÖSSER"

Hinge to fabric covered inspection panel
Fuel drain
Fuel sump
Wheel pant mount on D-IKNI. (pants not used)

On D-IKNI only
Not on D-IKNI.
Wheel covers glossy black

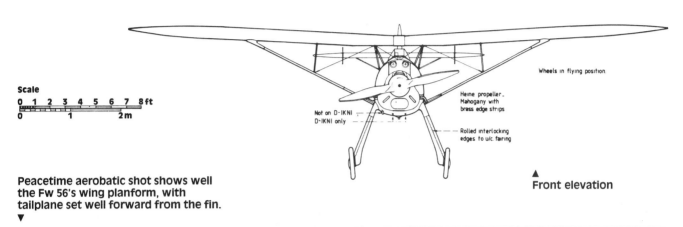

Wheels in flying position.

Heine propeller. Mahogany with brass edge strips

Not on D-IKNI
D-IKNI only

Rolled interlocking edges to u/c. fairing

**Scale**

0 1 2 3 4 5 6 7 8 ft

0     1     2m

▲
**Front elevation**

**Peacetime aerobatic shot shows well the Fw 56's wing planform, with tailplane set well forward from the fin.**
▼

# Polikarpov I-16

**Country of origin:** USSR.
**Type:** Single-seat, land-based fighter and fighter-bomber.
**Dimensions:** Wing span 29ft 6½in *9.00m*; length 20ft 1¼in *6.13m*; height 8ft 5in *2.57m*; wing area 161 sq ft *14.96m²*.
**Weights:** Empty 3285lb *1490kg*; normal loaded 4212lb *1910kg*; maximum 4547lb *2062kg*.
**Powerplant:** One Shvetsov M-62 nine-cylinder radial engine rated at 1000hp.
**Performance:** Maximum speed 326mph *525kph* at sea level; service ceiling 29,500ft *9000m*; range (max external fuel) 435 miles *700km*.
**Armament:** Two fixed 20mm ShVAK cannon and two fixed 7.62mm ShKAS machine guns, plus six 82mm RS82 rockets or equivalent load.
**Service:** First flight (prototype) December 1933; service entry late 1934.

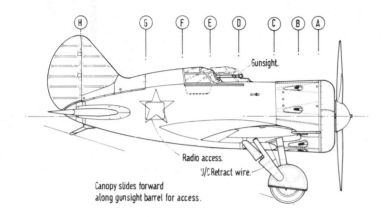

Gunsight.

Radio access.

'U/C Retract wire.

Canopy slides forward along gunsight barrel for access.

**Starboard elevation, Type 5** ▲

**DRAWN BY A A P LLOYD**

MARKINGS FOR
Nº 13 "Za USSR".

White.

ЗА СССР! ☆ Red.

13

Scale
0 1 2 3 4 5 6 7 8ft
0            1            2m

I-16s fought in the Spanish Civil War on both sides; this Type 6, powered by a 730hp M-25A, was one of a number supplied to the Republican Air Force. Note cockpit canopy slid into the aft position.
▼

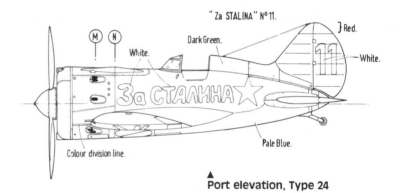

"Za STALINA" Nº 11.

} Red.

Dark Green.

White.

11

White.

За СТАЛИНА ☆

Pale Blue.

Colour division line.

**Port elevation, Type 24** ▲

▲
Type 6 in Nationalist markings, one of eighteen captured
from the Republicans. Canopy is slid forward in this view.

Fuselage cross-sections, Type 5
▼

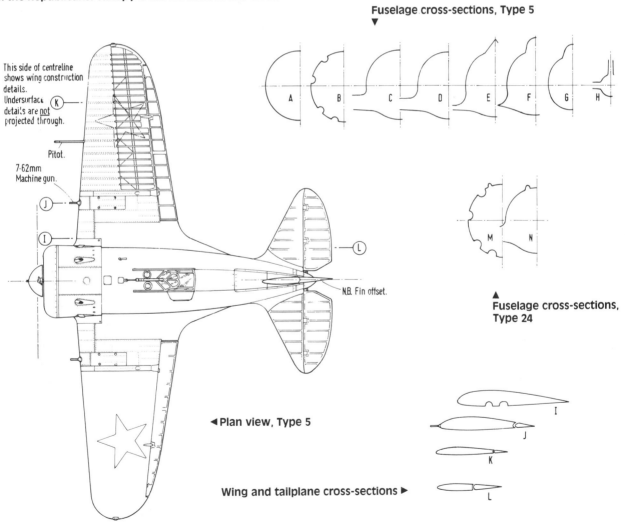

This side of centreline
shows wing construction
details.
Undersurface (K)
details are not
projected through.

Pitot.

7·62mm
Machine gun.

▲
Fuselage cross-sections,
Type 24

N.B. Fin offset.

◄Plan view, Type 5

Wing and tailplane cross-sections ►

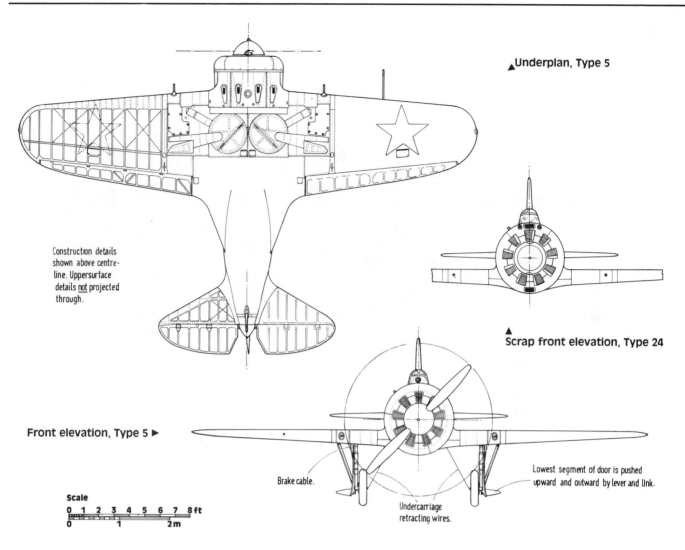

▲Underplan, Type 5

Construction details shown above centre-line. Uppersurface details not projected through.

▲
Scrap front elevation, Type 24

Front elevation, Type 5 ►

Brake cable.

Undercarriage retracting wires.

Lowest segment of door is pushed upward and outward by lever and link.

Scale
0 1 2 3 4 5 6 7 8 ft
0    1    2 m

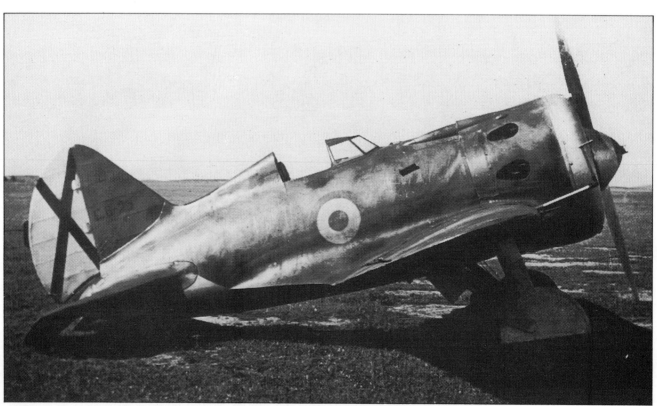

Advanced in concept when first introduced, the Soviet Air Force's I-16s were obsolete by 1941 but they nevertheless bore the brunt of the early *Luftwaffe* offensive during 'Barbarossa'. ▶

Scrap view (not to scale) ▶
*Instrument panel*

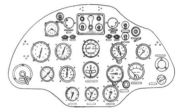

Typical ski installation, fixed position.

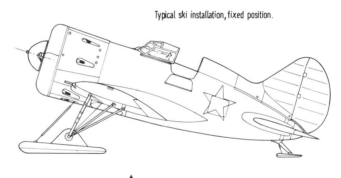

▲
Port elevation, Type 5

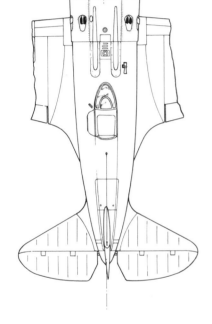

▲
Scrap plan view, Type 24

◀ I-16s were in service with the Spanish Air Force well into the 1950s and this photograph shows C.8-25, believed to be the last example on strength.

A poor-quality photo of a Soviet I-16 that has come to grief gives an idea of the slotted engine cowling and domed spinner. ▶

# Bücker Bü 133 Jungmeister

**Country of origin:** Germany.
**Type:** Single-seat, land-based advanced trainer.
**Dimensions:** Wing span 21ft 7½in *6.60m*; length 19ft 4in *5.90m*; height 7ft 4½in *2.25m*; wing area 129 sq ft *12.0m²*.

**Weights:** Empty 926lb *420kg*; loaded 1292lb *586kg*.
**Powerplant:** One Siemens Sh 14A-4 seven-cylinder radial engine rated at 160hp.
**Performance:** Maximum speed 134mph

*216kph*; initial climb rate 1170ft/min *355m/min*; service ceiling 20,000ft *6100m*; range 310 miles *500km*.
**Armament:** None.
**Service:** First flight 1935.

**Scale**

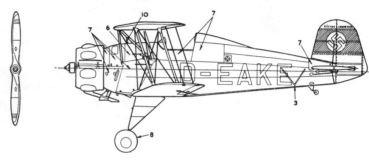

Port elevation, Prototype ►
*Sh 14A-4 engine*

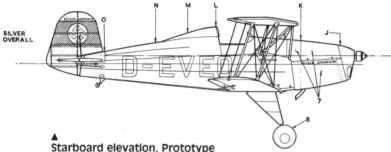

SILVER
OVERALL

▲
Starboard elevation, Prototype
*Hirth HM 506 engine*

**DRAWN BY G A G COX**

A classic by any standards, the Jungmeister is still a favoured aerobatic aircraft. This one sports a Swiss registration.
▼

▲
**Another Swiss-registered Bü 133, built by Dornier in 1940 and one of the subjects of our drawings.**

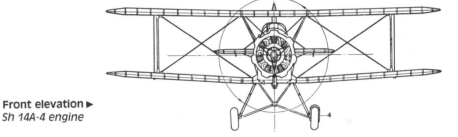

**Front elevation ▶**
*Sh 14A-4 engine*

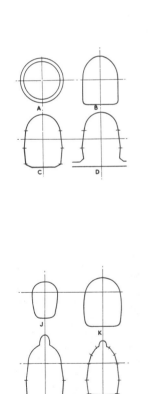

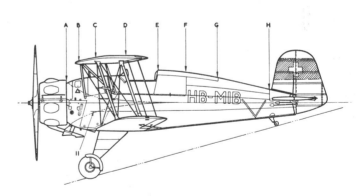

**Port elevation ▲**
*Sh 14A-4 engine*

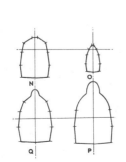

**◀ Fuselage cross-sections**

**Numerical key**
1. This strut port side only. 2. Black wing walk port side, all aircraft. 3. Zip fastener on inspection flap. 4. Mudguards often discarded. 5. Fabric lacing all along underside. 6. Petrol tank. 7. Metal panels. 8. Undercarriage in offload position. 9. No framing to this windshield. 10. Fuel gauge. 11. Colour lines. 12. Leather cuffs round interplane strut ends and tailwheel leg. 13. Leather crashpad. 14. Venturi tube. 15. Altimeter. 16. Clock. 17. Oil temperature. 18. Air speed indicator. 19. Accelerometer. 20. Engine rpm. 21. Oil pressure. 22. Fuel pressure. 23. Priming pump. 24. Toe brake pedal.

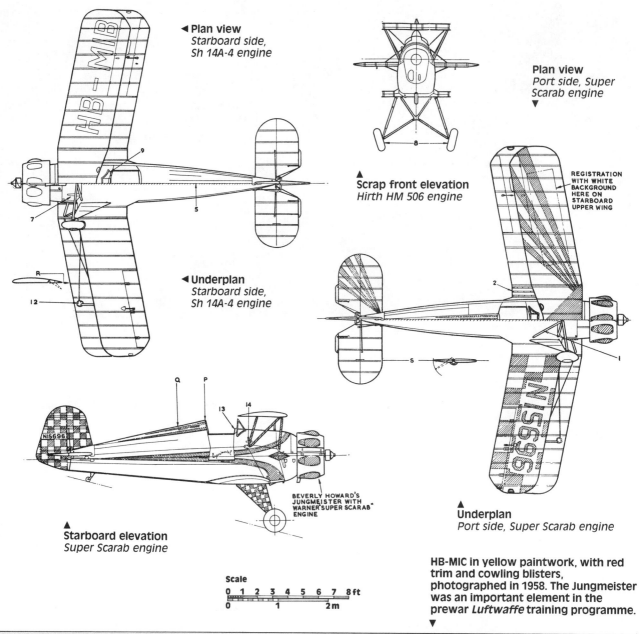

◄ **Plan view**
*Starboard side,
Sh 14A-4 engine*

**Plan view**
*Port side, Super
Scarab engine* ▼

9

7

5

R

12

▲ **Scrap front elevation**
*Hirth HM 506 engine*

8

REGISTRATION
WITH WHITE
BACKGROUND
HERE ON
STARBOARD
UPPER WING

◄ **Underplan**
*Starboard side,
Sh 14A-4 engine*

2

1

S

Q    P    13    14

BEVERLY HOWARD'S
JUNGMEISTER WITH
WARNER SUPER SCARAB
ENGINE

▲ **Underplan**
*Port side, Super Scarab engine*

▲ **Starboard elevation**
*Super Scarab engine*

**Scale**
0  1  2  3  4  5  6  7  8 ft
0              1              2 m

HB-MIC in yellow paintwork, with red
trim and cowling blisters,
photographed in 1958. The Jungmeister
was an important element in the
prewar *Luftwaffe* training programme.
▼

HB-MIC

▲
Count Cantacuzene's Jungmeister, well-known participant at aerobatic contests in the 1950s. Note rudder extension.

*Sketch section*

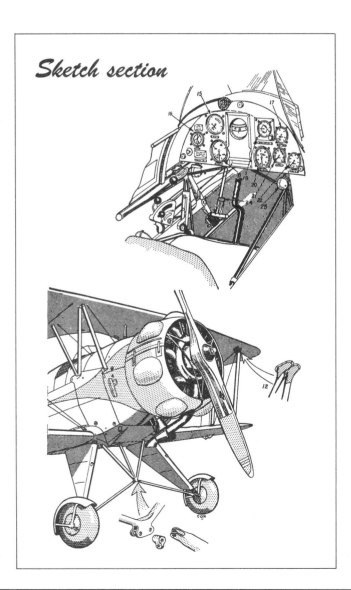

**Colour notes**
**HB-MIB:** Entire aircraft cream except for red cowl, fuselage trim and registrations. Red and white national rudder markings.
**D-EAKE:** Silver overall.
**D-EVEO:** Silver overall.
**N15696 (Beverly Howard's aircraft):** Entire aircraft white except for shaded areas (red); thin white then dark blue outline to fuselage markings. Handholds black.

Bü 133 instrument panel, considerably different from that depicted in the accompanying sketch and reflecting the 'customised' nature of privately owned Jungmeisters postwar.
▼

# Curtiss SBC-3 and -4 Helldiver

**Country of origin:** USA.
**Type:** Two-seat, carrier-based scout bomber.
**Dimensions:** Wing span 34ft 0in *10.36m*; length 27ft 5in *8.36m*; height 10ft 3½in *3.14m*; wing area 317 sq ft *29.45m²*.
**Weights:** Empty 4166lb *1889kg*, (-4) 4841lb *2195kg*; loaded 5581lb *2531kg*, (-4) 7632lb *3461kg*.

**Powerplant:** One Pratt & Whitney R-1535-94 Twin Wasp radial engine rated at 825hp, (-4) Wright R-1820-34 Cyclone rated at 950hp.
**Performance:** (-4) Maximum speed 235mph *378kph*; initial climb rate 1450ft/min *440m/min*; service ceiling 24,500ft *7470m*; range 610 miles *982km*.
**Armament:** One fixed 0.3in or 0.5in Colt

machine gun and one flexibly mounted 0.3in machine gun, plus one 500lb *227kg* or (-4) 1000lb *454kg* bomb beneath fuselage and one 100lb *45kg* bomb under each wing.
**Service:** First flight (XSBC-1) January 1934, (XSBC-3) March 1936; service entry (SBC-3) July 1937, (-4) 1938.

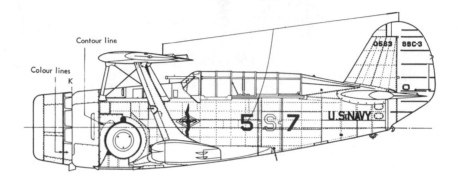

▲
Port elevation, SBC-3

---

### Colour notes

**SBC-3:** Tail surfaces, excluding fillets – red. Top surface of upper wing – chrome yellow. All other metal surfaces – light grey. Lower wings – silver. Engine cowling, wing chevron and fuselage band – blue with white border. VS-5 badge – black man o' war bird with red throat; red border to white diamond. White 'S', hyphens and tail lettering.
**XSBC-4:** Serial 0582. From station 'B' aft – as

SBC-4 except where indicated. Colour – all polished metal and silver dope, all lettering black.
**SBC-4:** Basic fuselage and wing colours as SBC-3. Tail, including fillets – blue (USS *Enterprise*). Cowl and fuselage bands – blue with white outline. Lettering – black (except white on tail). Carrier emblem – white disc with blue ship and surrounding circle.

---

The SBC was the last front-line military biplane to be produced in the USA, and was in service when war broke out in the Pacific. This is an SBC-4, powered by a 950hp Wright Cyclone.
▼

Close-in air-to-air view of an SBC-4, showing to advantage the streamlined centre-section strut fairings and retracted port main wheel. The immense width of the aircraft's ailerons is also apparent. ▶

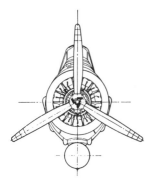

▲ Scrap front elevation, SBC-3
*Twin Wasp installation*

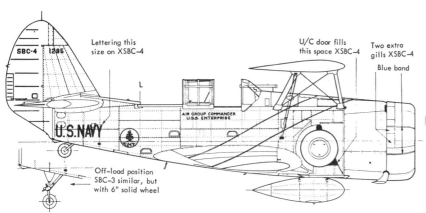

SBC-4 1295

Lettering this size on XSBC-4

L

AIR GROUP COMMANDER
U.S.S. ENTERPRISE

U.S. NAVY

Off-load position SBC-3 similar, but with 6" solid wheel

U/C door fills this space XSBC-4

Two extra gills XSBC-4

Blue band

▲ Starboard elevation, SBC-4

A number of SBC-4s on order for France were diverted to the RAF, where they were dubbed Clevelands. This one has a ground instructional serial number.
▼

**Scale**

0 1 2 3 4 5 6 7 8 ft
0 1 2 m

**Fuselage cross-sections**
▼

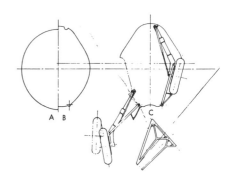

A B

C

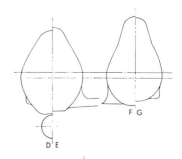

D E

F G

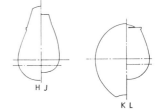

H J

K L

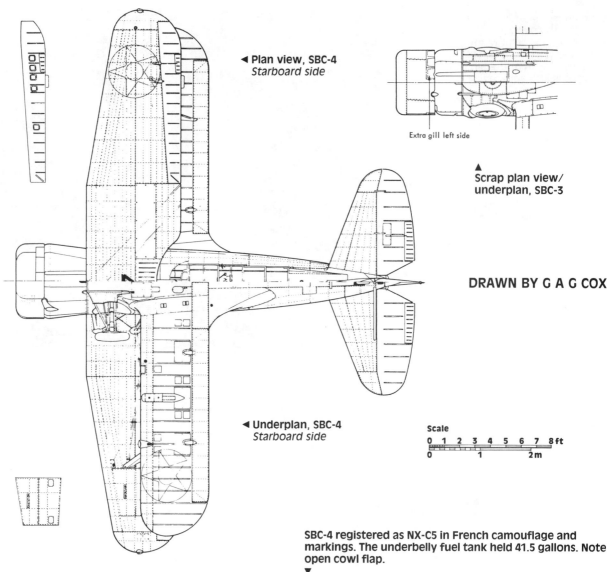

◄ **Plan view, SBC-4**
*Starboard side*

*Extra gill left side*

▲
**Scrap plan view/
underplan, SBC-3**

**DRAWN BY G A G COX**

◄ **Underplan, SBC-4**
*Starboard side*

Scale
0 1 2 3 4 5 6 7 8 ft
0          1          2 m

SBC-4 registered as NX-C5 in French camouflage and
markings. The underbelly fuel tank held 41.5 gallons. Note
open cowl flap.
▼

# Fieseler Fi 156C Storch

**Country of origin:** Germany.
**Type:** Three-seat, land-based communications, army co-operation and general-purpose aircraft.
**Dimensions:** Wing span 46ft 9in *14.25m*; length 32ft 6in *9.91m*; height 10ft 0in *3.05m*; wing area 279.9 sq ft *26.0m²*.

**Weights:** Empty 2051lb *930kg*; loaded 2924lb *1326kg*.
**Powerplant:** One Argus As 10C eight-cylinder, inverted-vee, air-cooled engine rated at 240hp.
**Performance:** Maximum speed 109mph *175kph* at sea level; time to 3000ft *915m*,

4min; service ceiling 16,700ft *5090m*; range 630 miles *1015km*.
**Armament:** One flexibly mounted 7.9mm MG 15 machine gun.
**Service:** First flight (V1) spring 1936; service entry (C-1) early 1939, (C-3) late 1940.

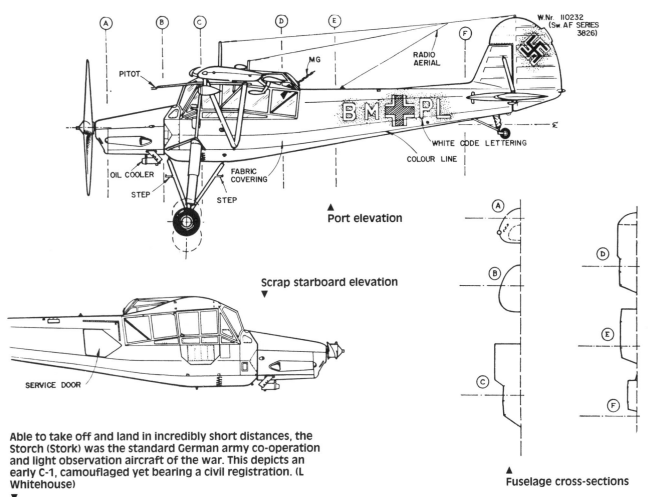

▲ Port elevation

Scrap starboard elevation
▼

▲ Fuselage cross-sections

Able to take off and land in incredibly short distances, the Storch (Stork) was the standard German army co-operation and light observation aircraft of the war. This depicts an early C-1, camouflaged yet bearing a civil registration. (L Whitehouse)
▼

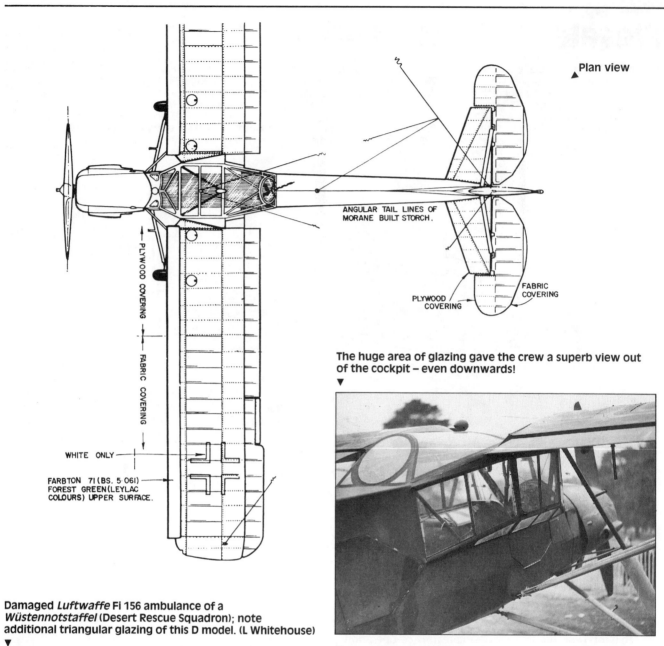

▲ Plan view

ANGULAR TAIL LINES OF
MORANE BUILT STORCH.

FABRIC
COVERING

PLYWOOD
COVERING

PLYWOOD COVERING

FABRIC COVERING

WHITE ONLY

FARBTON 71 (BS. 5·061)
FOREST GREEN (LEYLAC
COLOURS) UPPER SURFACE.

The huge area of glazing gave the crew a superb view out of the cockpit – even downwards!
▼

**Damaged** *Luftwaffe* **Fi 156 ambulance of a** *Wüstennotstaffel* **(Desert Rescue Squadron); note additional triangular glazing of this D model. (L Whitehouse)**
▼

▲
Storchs were produced in France as the MS.500 'Criquet' series; here an MS.502 fuselage awaits restoration work.

▲
Front cockpit detail of a WWII *Luftwaffe* Storch, showing compact instrument panel.

INVERTED SLAT NOT FITTED TO LATER VERSIONS

LACING

LACING

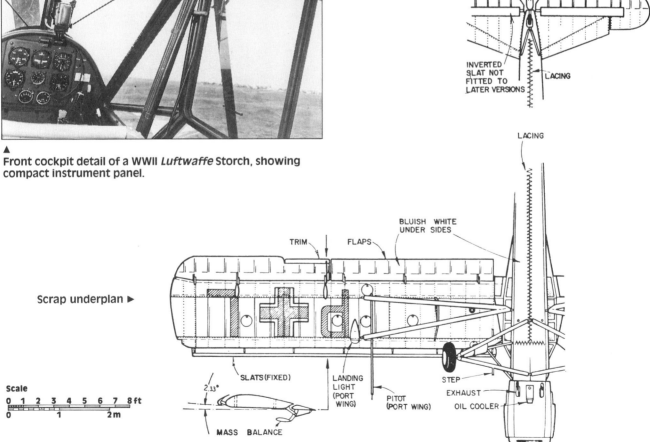

Scrap underplan ▶

TRIM
FLAPS
BLUISH WHITE UNDER SIDES

SLATS (FIXED)

2.33°

LANDING LIGHT (PORT WING)

PITOT (PORT WING)

STEP

EXHAUST

OIL COOLER

MASS BALANCE

Scale
0 1 2 3 4 5 6 7 8 ft
0       1         2 m

▲
**Fi 156C D-INBC again, here with wings folded back. Entire leading edge of wing was occupied by slots. (L Whitehouse)**

**Front elevation**
▼

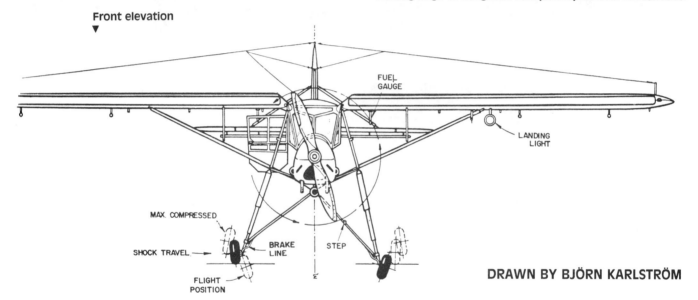

FUEL GAUGE

LANDING LIGHT

MAX. COMPRESSED

SHOCK TRAVEL

BRAKE LINE

STEP

FLIGHT POSITION

**DRAWN BY BJÖRN KARLSTRÖM**

◄ **VD+TD was one of several Storchs captured by the British and is seen here in the UK daubed as Air Ministry No 99. (IWM B6199)**

# Boeing-Stearman PT-13–18 Kaydet

**Country of origin:** USA.
**Type:** Two-seat, land-based primary trainer.
**Dimensions:** Wing span 32ft 2in *9.80m*; length 25ft 0¼in *7.63m*; height 9ft 2in *2.79m*; wing area 297.4 sq ft *27.63m²*.

**Weights:** Empty 1936lb *878kg*; loaded 2717lb *1232kg*.
**Powerplant:** One Lycoming R-680 radial engine rated at 220hp, (PT-17) Continental R-670 rated at 220hp, (PT-18) Jacobs R-755 rated at 225hp.

**Performance:** Maximum speed 124mph *200kph*; initial climb rate 840ft/min *256m/min*; service ceiling 11,200ft *3400m*; range 505 miles *813km*.
**Armament:** None.
**Service:** First flight: (PT-13) 1936.

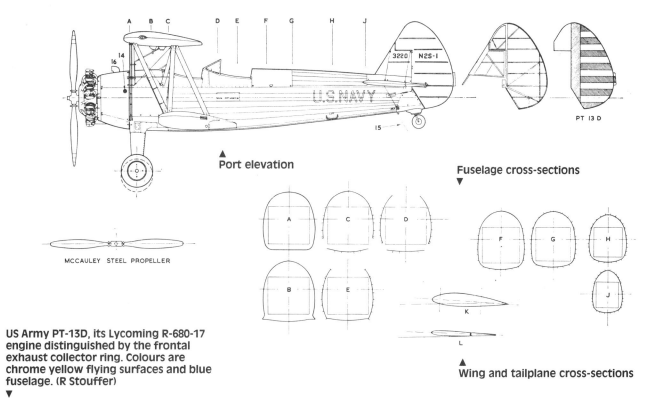

▲ Port elevation

Fuselage cross-sections ▼

PT 13 D

MCCAULEY STEEL PROPELLER

▲ Wing and tailplane cross-sections

US Army PT-13D, its Lycoming R-680-17 engine distinguished by the frontal exhaust collector ring. Colours are chrome yellow flying surfaces and blue fuselage. (R Stouffer) ▼

**DRAWN BY G A G COX**

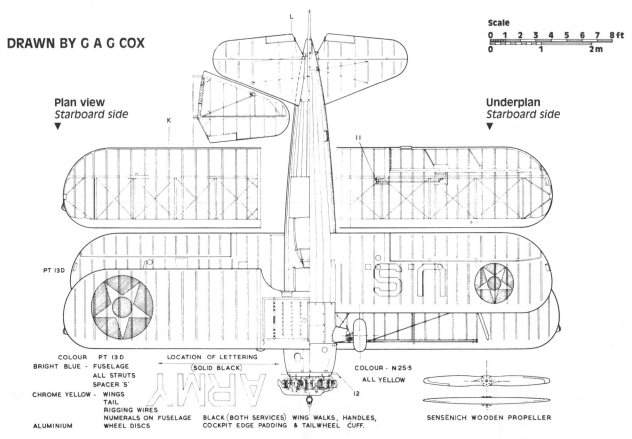

**Plan view**
*Starboard side*
▼

**Underplan**
*Starboard side*
▼

PT I3 D

**Scale**

0 1 2 3 4 5 6 7 8 ft

0      1      2m

COLOUR PT I3D
BRIGHT BLUE - FUSELAGE
ALL STRUTS
SPACER 'S'
CHROME YELLOW - WINGS
TAIL
RIGGING WIRES
NUMERALS ON FUSELAGE
ALUMINIUM    WHEEL DISCS

LOCATION OF LETTERING
(SOLID BLACK)

COLOUR - N2S-5
ALL YELLOW

BLACK (BOTH SERVICES) WING WALKS, HANDLES,
COCKPIT EDGE PADDING & TAILWHEEL CUFF.

SENSENICH WOODEN PROPELLER

▲
A Stearman N2S-3 in Navy markings. This model was the same as the N2S-1, except for the fitting of a later-model Continental R-670-4 engine. (R Stouffer)

US Navy N2S-4, with Continental engine, seen at the 1984 Annual Stearman Convention and fly-in, Galesburg, Illinois. (R Stouffer)
▼

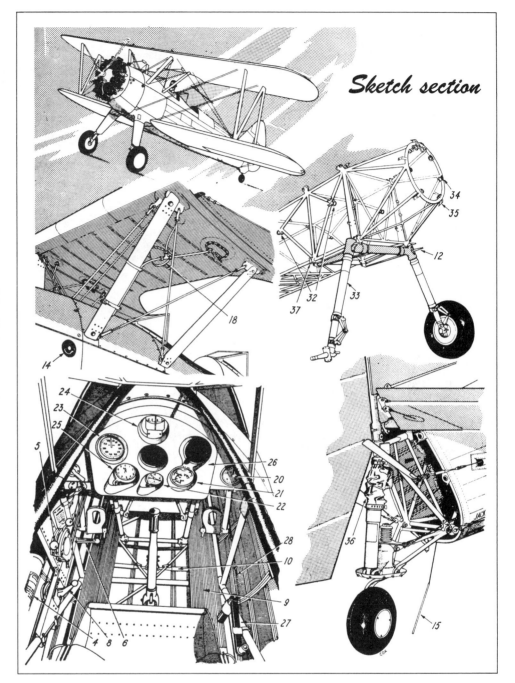

*Sketch section*

**Numerical key**
1. Firewall. 2. Baggage compartment. 3. Instrument panels. 4. Fire extinguisher. 5. Throttle. 6. Control lock lever. 7. Rudder pedal. 8. Elevator trim. 9. Corrugated heel boards. 10. Link rod to aileron crank. 11. Aileron crank. 12. Step. 13. Petrol filler cap. 14. Oil filler cap. 15. Static discharge rod. 16. Carburettor air intake. 17. Magneto switch operating rod. 18. Fuel gauge. 19. Elevator control tube. 20. Engine rpm. 21. Oil temperature and pressure. 22. Clock. 23. ASI. 24. Compass. 25. Altimeter. 26. Instrument panel, bevelled along sight lines. 27. Inertia starting handle (rear cockpit only). 28. Rudder cable. 29. Magneto switch. 30. Fuel cock. 31. Front seat. 32. Mounting lugs for pedals. 33. Complete undercarriage assembly detaches. 34. Engine mounting lugs. 35. Cowling attachment points. 36. Canvas cover. 37. Front spar mounting.

▲
PT-13 in US Army decor. The Boeing-
Stearman was the longest serving
biplane trainer, and many still fly today
for sport or as crop-dusters.
(M Passingham)

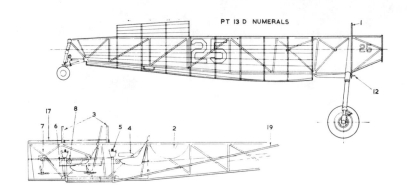

PT 13 D NUMERALS

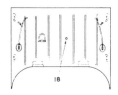

### Scrap underplan
*Upper wing centre-section*

### Scrap views ▲ ▶
*Showing internal structure*

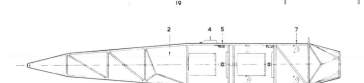

### Colour notes, PT-13D
Fuselage, all struts, spacers – bright blue.
Wings, tail, rigging wires, numerals on
fuselage – chrome yellow. Wheel discs –
aluminium. Wing walks, wing lettering,
handles, cockpit edge padding, tailwheel
cuff – black.

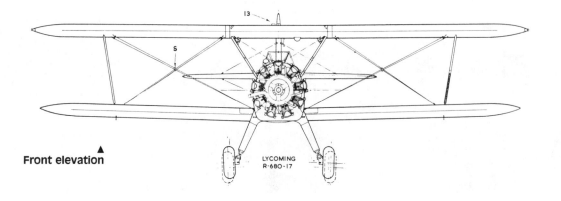

### Front elevation ▲

LYCOMING
R·680·17

# Fairey Seafox

**Country of origin:** Great Britain.
**Type:** Two-seat, ship-based light reconnaissance seaplane.
**Dimensions:** Wing span 40ft 0in *12.19m*; length 33ft 5½in *10.20m*; height 12ft 2in *3.71m*; wing area 434 sq ft *40.32m²*.
**Weights:** Empty 3805lb *1726kg*; loaded 5420lb *2458kg*; max catapulting 5650lb *2562kg*.
**Powerplant:** One Napier Rapier VI sixteen-cylinder, H type, air-cooled engine rated at 395hp.
**Performance:** Maximum speed 124mph *199.6kph*; initial climb rate 420ft/min *130m/min*; service ceiling 9700ft *2950m*; range 440 miles *710km*.
**Armament:** One flexibly mounted 0.303in Lewis machine gun.
**Service:** First flight (prototype) 27 May 1936; service entry 23 April 1937.

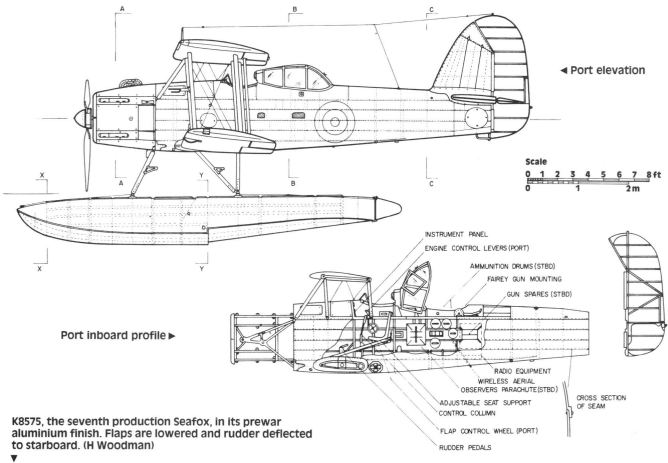

◀ Port elevation

Scale

Port inboard profile ▶

INSTRUMENT PANEL
ENGINE CONTROL LEVERS (PORT)
AMMUNITION DRUMS (STBD)
FAIREY GUN MOUNTING
GUN SPARES (STBD)
RADIO EQUIPMENT
WIRELESS AERIAL
OBSERVERS PARACHUTE (STBD)
ADJUSTABLE SEAT SUPPORT
CONTROL COLUMN
CROSS SECTION
OF SEAM
FLAP CONTROL WHEEL (PORT)
RUDDER PEDALS

K8575, the seventh production Seafox, in its prewar aluminium finish. Flaps are lowered and rudder deflected to starboard. (H Woodman)
▼

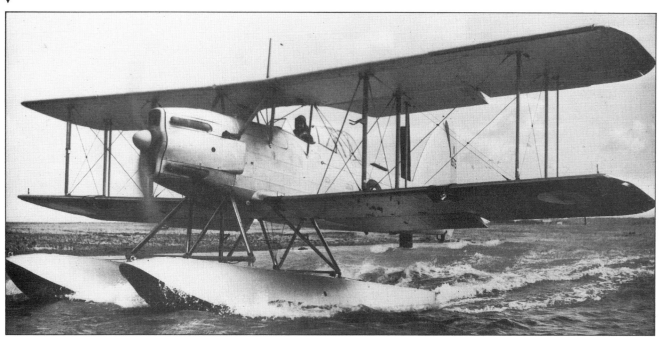

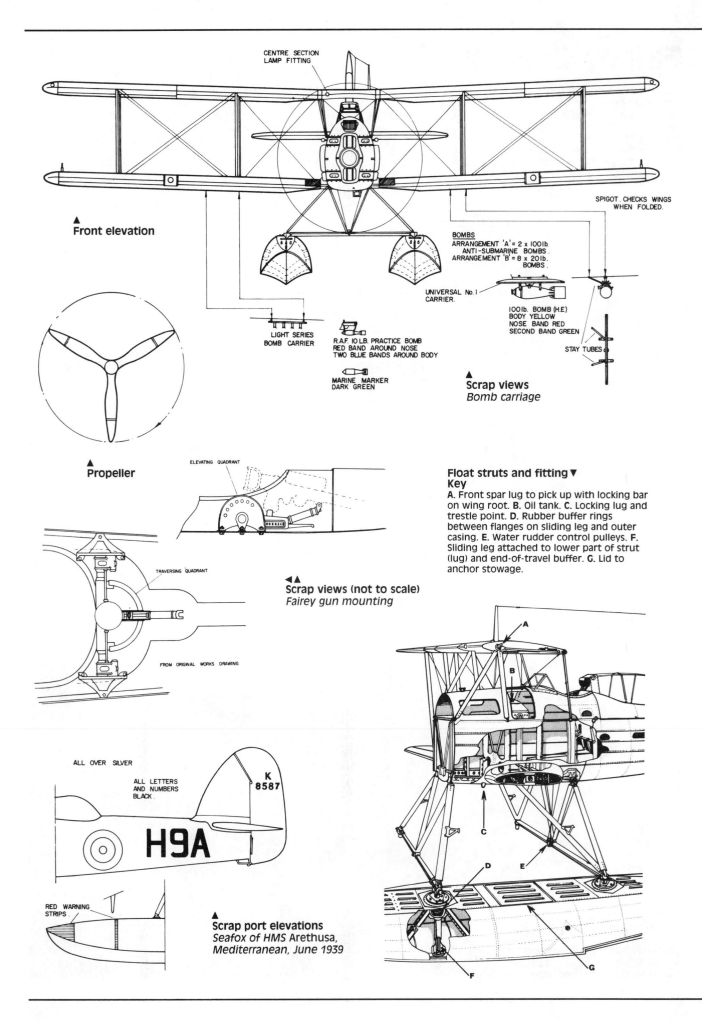

CENTRE SECTION
LAMP FITTING

▲ **Front elevation**

SPIGOT. CHECKS WINGS
WHEN FOLDED.

BOMBS
ARRANGEMENT 'A' = 2 x 100 lb.
ANTI-SUBMARINE BOMBS.
ARRANGEMENT 'B' = 8 x 20 lb.
BOMBS.

UNIVERSAL No.1
CARRIER.

100 lb. BOMB (H.E)
BODY YELLOW
NOSE BAND RED
SECOND BAND GREEN

STAY TUBES

LIGHT SERIES
BOMB CARRIER

R.A.F. 10 LB. PRACTICE BOMB
RED BAND AROUND NOSE
TWO BLUE BANDS AROUND BODY

MARINE MARKER
DARK GREEN

▲ **Scrap views**
*Bomb carriage*

▲ **Propeller**

ELEVATING QUADRANT

TRAVERSING QUADRANT

FROM ORIGINAL WORKS DRAWING

◄▲ **Scrap views (not to scale)**
*Fairey gun mounting*

### Float struts and fitting ▼
### Key
**A.** Front spar lug to pick up with locking bar on wing root. **B.** Oil tank. **C.** Locking lug and trestle point. **D.** Rubber buffer rings between flanges on sliding leg and outer casing. **E.** Water rudder control pulleys. **F.** Sliding leg attached to lower part of strut (lug) and end-of-travel buffer. **G.** Lid to anchor stowage.

ALL OVER SILVER

ALL LETTERS
AND NUMBERS
BLACK.

K
8587

H9A

RED WARNING
STRIPS

▲ **Scrap port elevations**
*Seafox of HMS Arethusa, Mediterranean, June 1939*

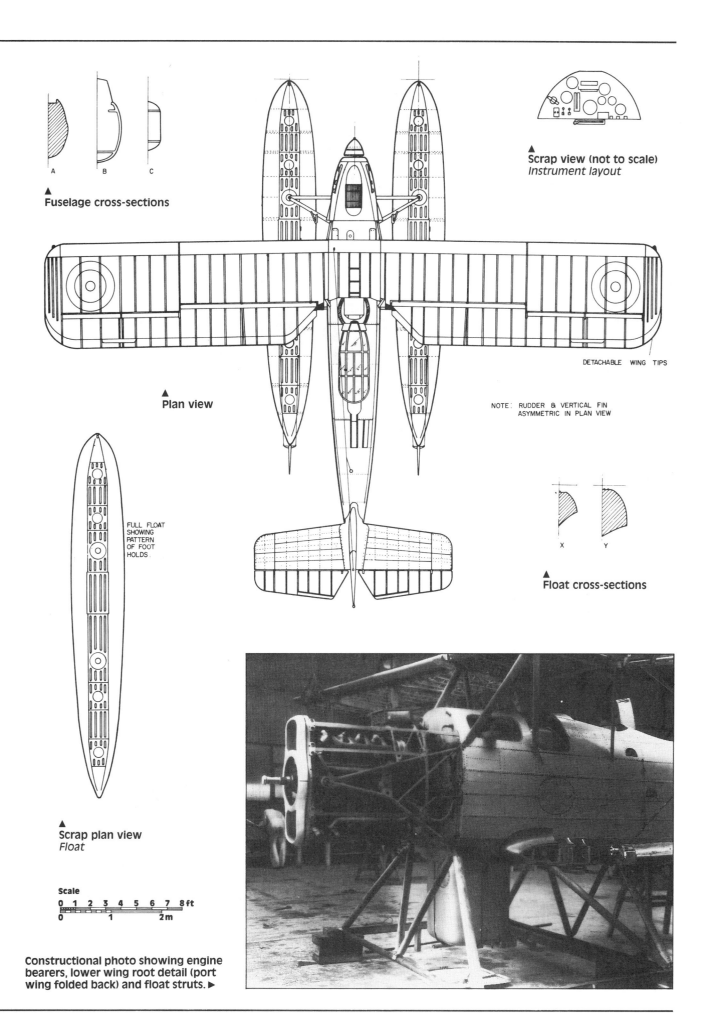

▲
**Fuselage cross-sections**

A    B    C

▲
**Scrap view (not to scale)**
*Instrument layout*

▲
**Plan view**

DETACHABLE WING TIPS

NOTE: RUDDER & VERTICAL FIN
ASYMMETRIC IN PLAN VIEW

FULL FLOAT
SHOWING
PATTERN
OF FOOT
HOLDS

X    Y

▲
**Float cross-sections**

▲
**Scrap plan view**
*Float*

**Scale**

0  1  2  3  4  5  6  7  8 ft
0          1          2 m

**Constructional photo showing engine
bearers, lower wing root detail (port
wing folded back) and float struts.** ▶

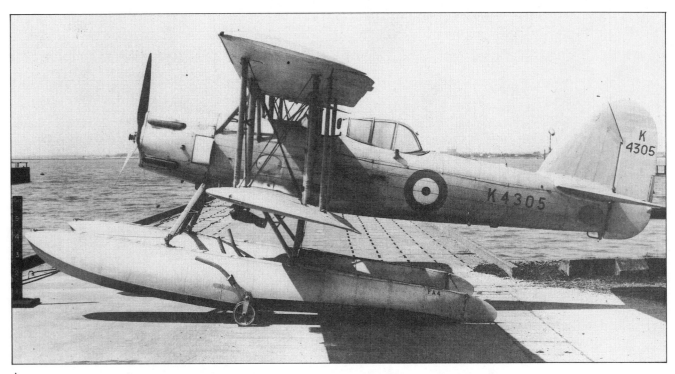

▲
The second prototype Seafox photographed on its beaching gear during testing at Felixstowe. Note the stylistic variations in the presentation of the serial numbers on fuselage and fin. (H Woodman)

**DRAWN BY HARRY WOODMAN**

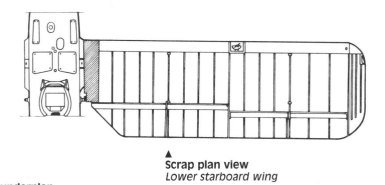

▲
**Scrap plan view**
*Lower starboard wing*

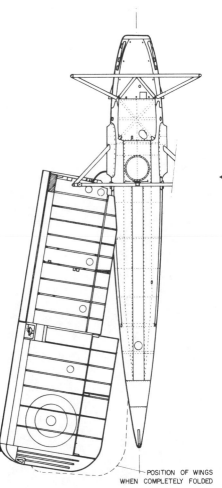

◄ Scrap underplan

POSITION OF WINGS
WHEN COMPLETELY FOLDED

Lower starboard wing prior to covering, showing metal-sheathed leading edge and flap and aileron hinge lines.
▼

# Westland Lysander Mks I, II and IIIA

**Country of origin:** Great Britain.
**Type:** Two-seat, land-based army co-operation and general-purpose aircraft.
**Dimensions:** Wing span 50ft 0in *15.24m*; length 30ft 6in *9.30m*; height 14ft 6in *4.42m*; wing area 260 sq ft *24.15m²*.
**Weights:** Empty 4365lb *1980kg*; loaded

6318lb *2865kg*.
**Powerplant:** One Bristol Mercury XII nine-cylinder radial engine rated at 890hp, (Mk II) Perseus XII rated at 905hp, (Mk III) Mercury XX or XXX rated at 870hp, (Mk IIIA) Mercury XXX rated at 870hp.
**Performance:** Maximum speed 212mph *341kph* at 5000ft *1525m*; initial climb rate

1410ft/min *430m/min*; service ceiling 21,500ft *6550m*.
**Armament:** Two fixed 0.303in Browning machine guns and one flexibly mounted Vickers K gun, plus up to six light bombs.
**Service:** First flight (prototype) 15 June 1936; service entry (Mk I) late 1938.

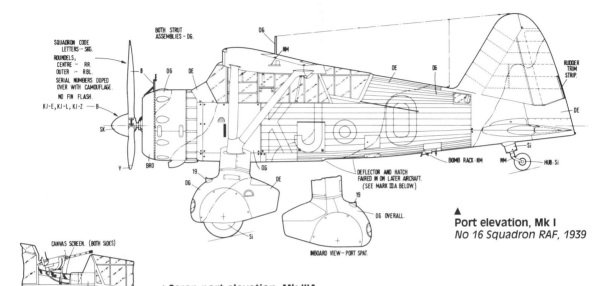

▲ **Port elevation, Mk I**
*No 16 Squadron RAF, 1939*

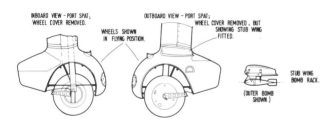

◀ **Scrap port elevation, Mk IIIA**
*Gunner's cockpit*

**Scrap views**
*Undercarriage spats*
▼

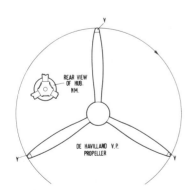

▲ **Propeller details**

Prewar shot of a trio of Lysanders peeling off for the camera, the shape of the tailplanes identifying the machines as Mk IIs. The camouflage patterns of the two nearest aircraft are 'mirror images' of each other.
▼

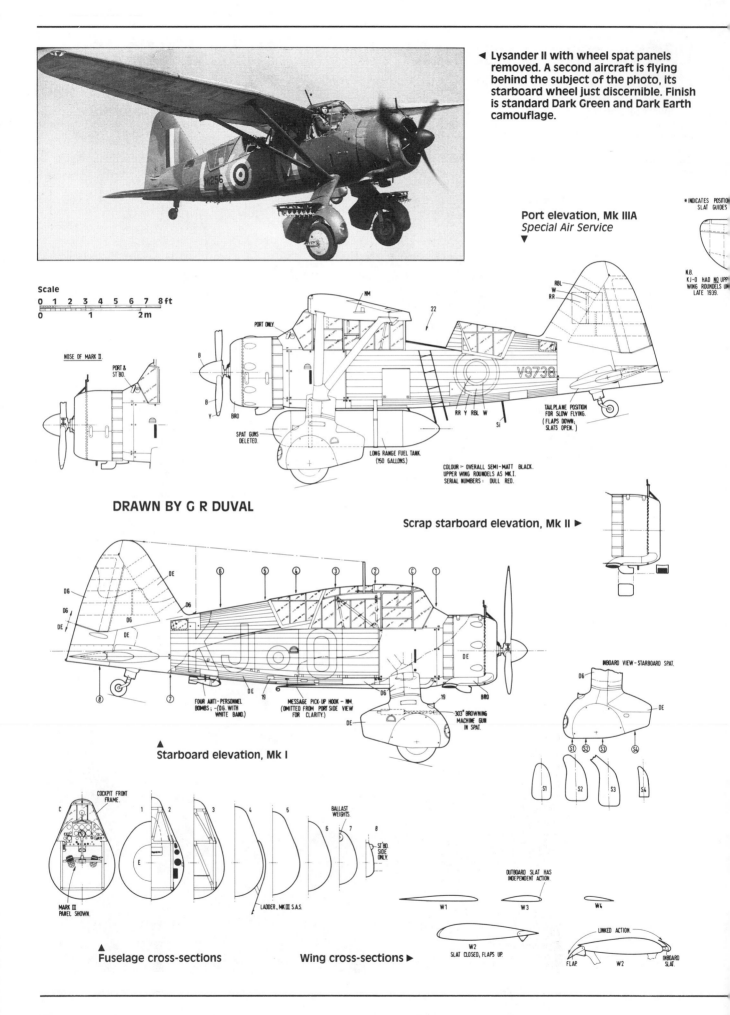

◀ Lysander II with wheel spat panels removed. A second aircraft is flying behind the subject of the photo, its starboard wheel just discernible. Finish is standard Dark Green and Dark Earth camouflage.

Port elevation, Mk IIIA
*Special Air Service*
▼

\* INDICATES POSITION SLAT GUIDES

N.B.
KJ-O HAD NO UPPER WING ROUNDELS UNTIL LATE 1939.

Scale
0 1 2 3 4 5 6 7 8 ft
0 1 2 m

NOSE OF MARK II.

PORT & ST'BD.

PORT ONLY.

NM

22

RBL
W
RR

B

B

Y

BRO

V9738

SPAT GUNS DELETED.

LONG RANGE FUEL TANK. (150 GALLONS.)

RR Y RBL W

Si

TAILPLANE POSITION FOR SLOW FLYING. ( FLAPS DOWN; SLATS OPEN. )

COLOUR :- OVERALL SEMI-MATT BLACK.
UPPER WING ROUNDELS AS MK.I.
SERIAL NUMBERS : DULL RED.

DRAWN BY G R DUVAL

Scrap starboard elevation, Mk II ▶

DE

DG

DG

DE

DG

DG

DE

DE

⑥ ⑤ ④ ③ ② Ⓒ ①

KJ-O

DE

⑧ ⑦

DE

19

FOUR ANTI-PERSONNEL BOMBS ; -(DG. WITH WHITE BAND.)

MESSAGE PICK-UP HOOK - NM. (OMITTED FROM PORT SIDE VIEW FOR CLARITY.)

DE

DG

19

BRO

303ª BROWNING MACHINE GUN IN SPAT.

DE

▲
Starboard elevation, Mk I

INBOARD VIEW - STARBOARD SPAT.

DG

DE

S1 S2 S3 S4

S1 S2 S3 S4

COCKPIT FRONT FRAME.

C 1 2 3 4 5

BALLAST WEIGHTS.

6 7 8

ST'BD. SIDE ONLY.

E

MARK III PANEL SHOWN.

LADDER , MK III S.A.S.

OUTBOARD SLAT HAS INDEPENDENT ACTION.

W1 W3 W4

▲
Fuselage cross-sections

Wing cross-sections ▶

W2
SLAT CLOSED, FLAPS UP.

LINKED ACTION.

FLAP W2 INBOARD SLAT.

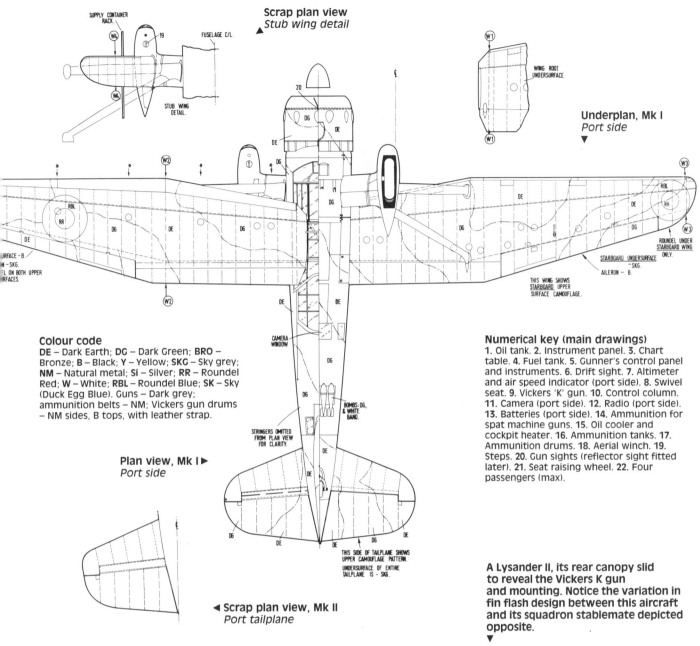

**Scrap plan view**
*Stub wing detail* ▲

SUPPLY CONTAINER RACK.

19

FUSELAGE C/L.

STUB WING DETAIL.

**Underplan, Mk I**
*Port side* ▼

WING ROOT UNDERSURFACE

RBL

RR

ROUNDEL UNDER STARBOARD WING ONLY.

STARBOARD UNDERSURFACE – SKG.

AILERON – B.

THIS WING SHOWS STARBOARD UPPER SURFACE CAMOUFLAGE.

CAMERA WINDOW

BOMBS: DG, & WHITE BAND.

STRINGERS OMITTED FROM PLAN VIEW FOR CLARITY.

THIS SIDE OF TAILPLANE SHOWS UPPER CAMOUFLAGE PATTERN.
UNDERSURFACE OF ENTIRE TAILPLANE IS – SKG.

**Plan view, Mk I** ▶
*Port side*

◀ **Scrap plan view, Mk II**
*Port tailplane*

## Colour code

**DE** – Dark Earth; **DG** – Dark Green; **BRO** – Bronze; **B** – Black; **Y** – Yellow; **SKG** – Sky grey; **NM** – Natural metal; **Si** – Silver; **RR** – Roundel Red; **W** – White; **RBL** – Roundel Blue; **SK** – Sky (Duck Egg Blue). Guns – Dark grey; ammunition belts – NM; Vickers gun drums – NM sides, B tops, with leather strap.

## Numerical key (main drawings)

**1.** Oil tank. **2.** Instrument panel. **3.** Chart table. **4.** Fuel tank. **5.** Gunner's control panel and instruments. **6.** Drift sight. **7.** Altimeter and air speed indicator (port side). **8.** Swivel seat. **9.** Vickers 'K' gun. **10.** Control column. **11.** Camera (port side). **12.** Radio (port side). **13.** Batteries (port side). **14.** Ammunition for spat machine guns. **15.** Oil cooler and cockpit heater. **16.** Ammunition tanks. **17.** Ammunition drums. **18.** Aerial winch. **19.** Steps. **20.** Gun sights (reflector sight fitted later). **21.** Seat raising wheel. **22.** Four passengers (max).

A Lysander II, its rear canopy slid to reveal the Vickers K gun and mounting. Notice the variation in fin flash design between this aircraft and its squadron stablemate depicted opposite.
▼

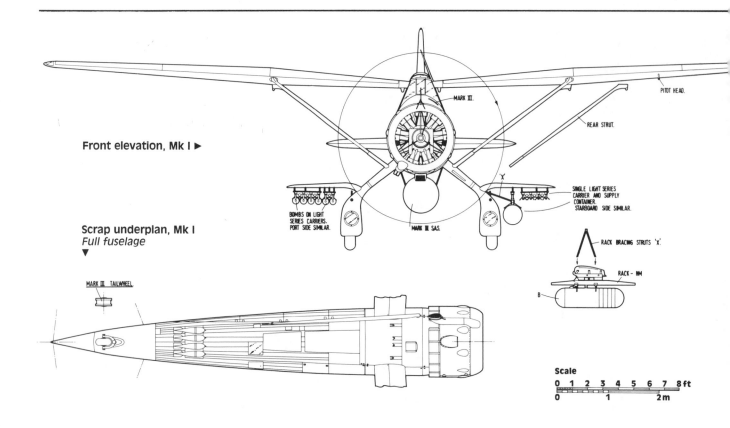

Front elevation, Mk I ▶

Scrap underplan, Mk I
*Full fuselage*
▼

MARK III.

PITOT HEAD.

REAR STRUT.

SINGLE LIGHT SERIES
CARRIER AND SUPPLY
CONTAINER.
STARBOARD SIDE SIMILAR.

BOMBS ON LIGHT
SERIES CARRIERS.
PORT SIDE SIMILAR.

'X'

MARK III S.A.S.

MARK III TAILWHEEL

RACK BRACING STRUTS 'X'.

RACK - NM

B

Scale
0 1 2 3 4 5 6 7 8 ft
0           1           2 m

The fuselage structure laid bare, showing the U-section gusset plates forward and welded steel-tubing construction aft. Wooden stringers, not present here, formed the framework for the fabric covering.
▼

Close up views showing (clockwise from top left) starboard wheel spat and landing light; port wing strut attachment; exhaust pipe detail; and pilot's cockpit glazing, port side. ▶

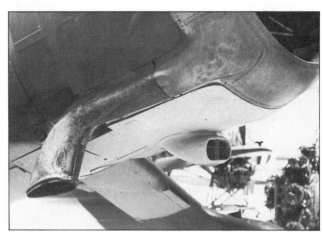

## Sketch section

### Key to cockpit and armament sketches

1. Aerial winch (trailing aerial). 2. Barrel lock for machine gun. 3. Spare ammunition containers. 4. Swivelling seat. 5. Chart table (fuel tank below). 6. Radio. 7. Camera. 8. Battery. 9. Pilot's seat pan (natural metal). 10. Fuel pressure (green). 11. Oil pressure (yellow). 12. Boost-manifold pressure (red rim). 13. Ammeter. 14. Rev counter (black rim). 15. Compass lamp switch. 16. Pilot's services switches. 17. Push button for gunner's warning lamp. 18. Morse key. 19. Cowl gills control. 20. Seat raising wheel. 21. TR9 radio control (Mk I only). 22. Side window retracted. 23. Leather padding. 24. Tailplane trimmer control. 25. Radio socket for helmet lead. 26. Engine primer pump. 27. Engine starting panel. 28. Engine priming cock. 29. Engine data plate. 30. Air intake control. 31. Cockpit heating control. 32. Oil warming control. 33. Oil temperature (yellow rim). 34. Carburettor air control. 35. Rudder bar adjustment. 36. Control column (with brake lever and gun button). 37. Propeller pitch control. 38. Throttle lever. 39. Mixture control. 40. VHF radio selector. 41. Landing lamp switch. 42. Fuel cock. 43. Fuel gauge. 44. Oxygen control. 45. Ignition switches. 46. Air pressure gauge. 47. Flare switch. 48. Rear gun sight. 49. Rudder pedals. 50. Mount for reflector sight. 51. Compass. 52. Mounting position for eight Very light cartridges. 53. Bomb selector switches. 54. Bomb release lever and jettison switch. 55. Clock.

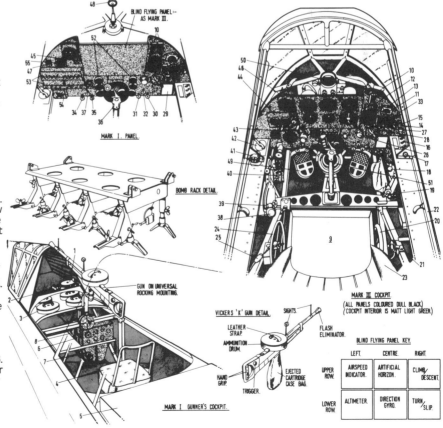

BLIND FLYING PANEL:— AS MARK III.

MARK I. PANEL.

BOMB RACK DETAIL.

GUN ON UNIVERSAL ROCKING MOUNTING.

MARK I GUNNER'S COCKPIT.

VICKERS 'K' GUN DETAIL.

SIGHTS.
LEATHER STRAP.
FLASH ELIMINATOR.
AMMUNITION DRUM.
HAND GRIP.
EJECTED CARTRIDGE CASE BAG.
TRIGGER.

MARK III COCKPIT.
(ALL PANELS COLOURED DULL BLACK.)
(COCKPIT INTERIOR IS MATT LIGHT GREEN.)

BLIND FLYING PANEL KEY.

|  | LEFT | CENTRE | RIGHT |
|---|---|---|---|
| UPPER ROW. | AIRSPEED INDICATOR. | ARTIFICIAL HORIZON. | CLIMB/DESCENT. |
| LOWER ROW. | ALTIMETER. | DIRECTION GYRO. | TURN/SLIP. |

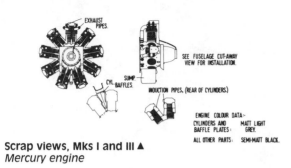

EXHAUST PIPES.

CYL. BAFFLES

SUMP.

SEE FUSELAGE CUT-AWAY VIEW FOR INSTALLATION.

INDUCTION PIPES, (REAR OF CYLINDERS.)

ENGINE COLOUR DATA:-
CYLINDERS AND     MATT LIGHT
BAFFLE PLATES:     GREY.

ALL OTHER PARTS:    SEMI-MATT BLACK.

**Scrap views, Mks I and III ▲**
*Mercury engine*

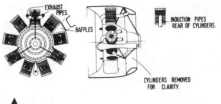

EXHAUST PIPES.

BAFFLES

INDUCTION PIPES REAR OF CYLINDERS.

CYLINDERS REMOVED FOR CLARITY.

▲
**Scrap views, Mk II**
*Perseus engine*

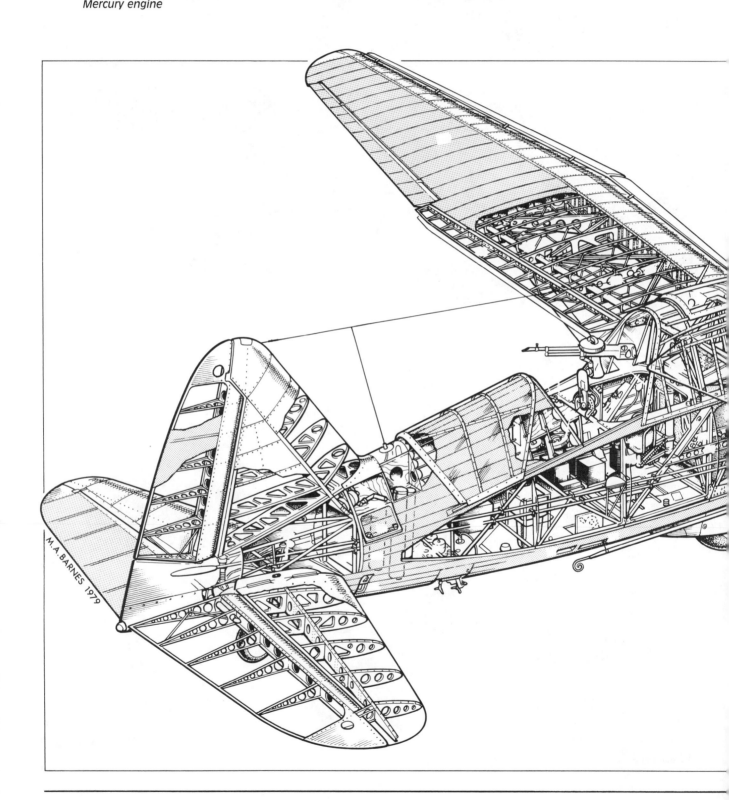

M.A.BARNES 1979

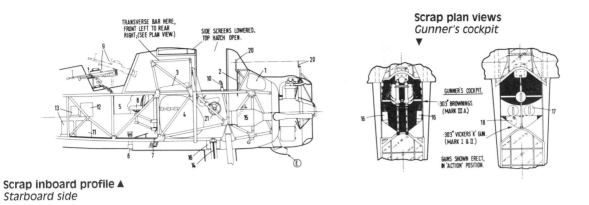

**Scrap plan views**
*Gunner's cockpit*
▼

GUNNER'S COCKPIT.

·303" BROWNINGS.
(MARK III A)

·303" VICKERS 'K' GUN
(MARK I & II.)

GUNS SHOWN ERECT,
IN 'ACTION' POSITION.

**Scrap inboard profile** ▲
*Starboard side*

**Cutaway drawing**
*By Tony Barnes*

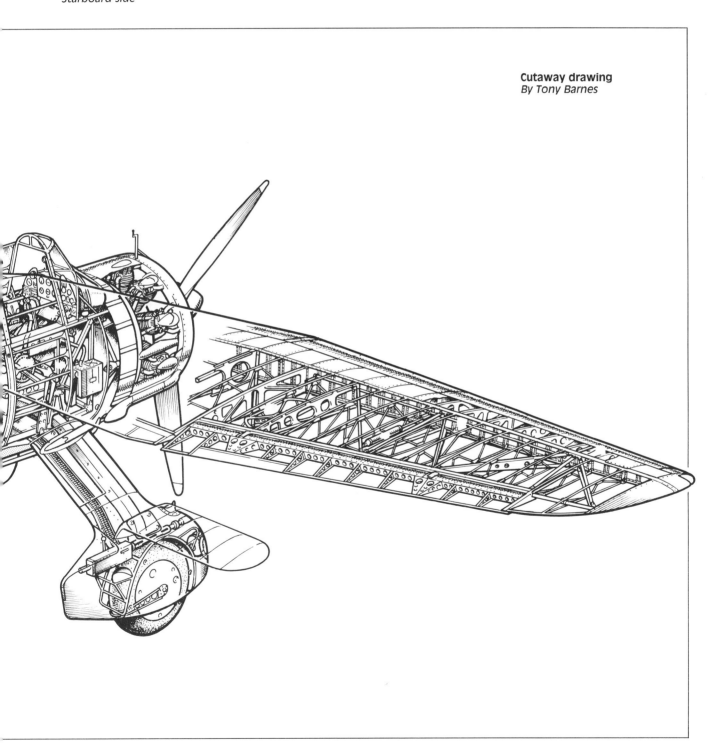

# Piper J3C Cub

**Country of origin**: USA.
**Type**: Two-seat, land-based trainer.
**Dimensions**: Wing span 35ft 2½in *10.73m*; length 22ft 4½in *6.82m*; height 6ft 8in *2.03m*; wing area 178.5 sq ft *16.58m²*.

**Weights**: Empty 680lb *308kg*; loaded 1220lb *553kg*.
**Powerplant**: One Continental, Lycoming or Franklin four-cylinder, horizontally opposed engine rated at 65hp.
**Performance**: Maximum speed 87mph

*140kph*; initial climb rate 450ft/min *135m/min*; service ceiling 11,500ft *3500m*; range 206 miles *330km*.
**Armament**: None.
**Service**: First flight (J3) late 1937.

**Port elevation ▶**

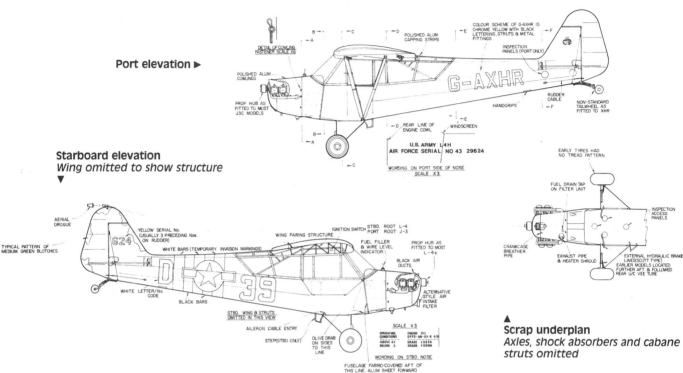

**Starboard elevation**
*Wing omitted to show structure*
▼

**▲ Scrap underplan**
*Axles, shock absorbers and cabane struts omitted*

The Cub family represented one of the most popular light aircraft designs of all time, the basic 40hp version originally selling for a mere $995! This is a US Army L-4. (M Brett)
▼

**DRAWN BY MAURICE BRETT**

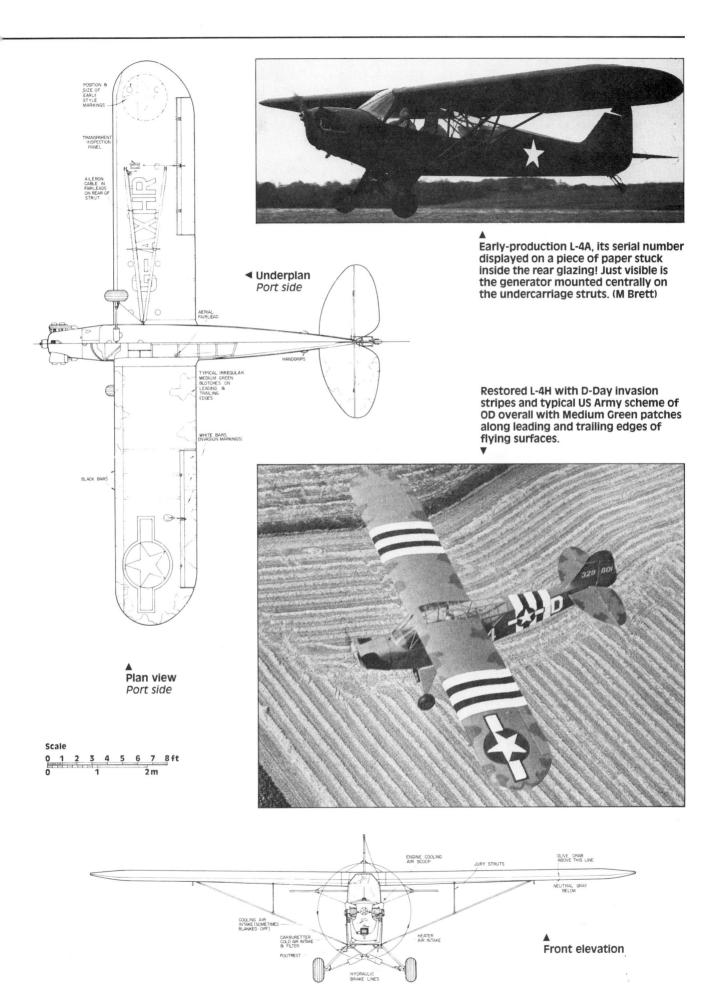

POSITION & SIZE OF EARLY STYLE MARKINGS

TRANSPARENT INSPECTION PANEL

AILERON CABLE IN FAIRLEADS ON REAR OF STRUT

◄ **Underplan**
*Port side*

AERIAL FAIRLEAD

HANDGRIPS

TYPICAL IRREGULAR MEDIUM GREEN BLOTCHES ON LEADING & TRAILING EDGES

WHITE BARS (INVASION MARKINGS)

BLACK BARS

▲ **Plan view**
*Port side*

**Scale**

```
0  1  2  3  4  5  6  7  8 ft
0           1           2 m
```

▲
**Early-production L-4A, its serial number displayed on a piece of paper stuck inside the rear glazing! Just visible is the generator mounted centrally on the undercarriage struts. (M Brett)**

**Restored L-4H with D-Day invasion stripes and typical US Army scheme of OD overall with Medium Green patches along leading and trailing edges of flying surfaces.**
▼

ENGINE COOLING AIR SCOOP

JURY STRUTS

OLIVE DRAB ABOVE THIS LINE

NEUTRAL GRAY BELOW

COOLING AIR INTAKE (SOMETIMES BLANKED OFF)

CARBURETTER COLD AIR INTAKE & FILTER

FOOTREST

HEATER AIR INTAKE

HYDRAULIC BRAKE LINES

▲ **Front elevation**

Aerial fairlead · Aerial winch · Radio panel · Headset · Tail trim winder · Vertical sliding window panel · Fuel cock control · Throttle lever (2) · Instruments · Fuel filler

Radio · Fuel tank · Fuel cock · Fuel supply to filter & engine · Front rudder pedal

G · Tail trim cables · Elevator control cables · Rudder cable · Ply footboards · Seat belt clips · Back support strap (fwd. position shown dotted) · Control assembly mounting bracket · Elevator control crank · Aileron control crank · Carb heat control (stbd only) · Rear brake pedal · Rear brake pedal & lever · Scott type brake cylinder · Optional generator · G · Front rudder pedal

Ply chart board · Radio · Seat pan · Throttle lever · Rear brake pedal · Ply floor with alum kick plates

Elevator cables · Front brake pedal · Front rudder pedal

Rudder cable · Seat support tubes · Alum conical cover over aileron cable · Rear rudder pedal · Brake cylinder · Brake operating lever

SECTION ON G–G PART CUT-AWAY TO SHOW FLOOR LEVEL FITTINGS

▲ **Scrap views** *Interior details*

## Fuselage cross-sections
▼

Exhaust manifold · Engine mount · Air heater shroud · Heater air intake pipes · Cabin heater & ventilator · Exhaust pipe · Carb heat supply · A–A

Rev counter · A.S.I. · Compass · Altimeter · Cabin heat · Oil temp · Oil press · Primer · Fuel tank · Fuel cock & control · Brake or lever · Cabin heater inlet · Front rudder pedal · Brake pedal · B–B

Wingspar · Front wing attachment · Throttle levers · Tail trim winder · Rear rudder pedal · Brake cylinder · Brake pedal · C–C

Rear wing attachment · Fabric · Aerial fairlead · Wingspar · Clips for control column stowage · Aerial winch · Optional radio · Harness attachment · Chart board shelf · Seat pan · Fabric covering · Rear seat support · Rudder cable fairlead · Ply footboards · D–D · Elevator control lever · Back support strap

E–E · F–F

Screw jack · Tailplane yoke · Tailplane L.E. · Cable tensioner & jockey pulley · Trimmer cables

ENLARGED VIEW ON TAIL TRIM CONTROL MECHANISM SEE SECTION F–F

**Piper O-59 Cub photographed in May 1943. Early civilian Cubs had less extensive glazing, and none at all above the heads of the crew. (Crown Copyright)**
▼

Scale

0 1 2 3 4 5 6 7 8 ft

0 · 1 · 2 m

## Wing cross-sections
▼

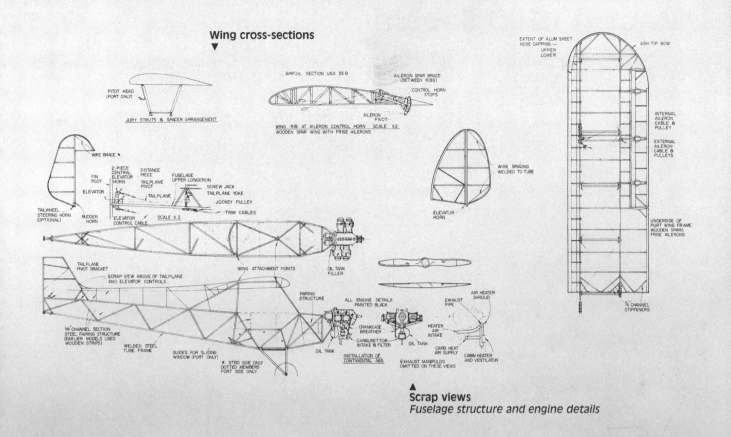

PITOT HEAD (PORT ONLY)

JURY STRUTS & SPACER ARRANGEMENT

AIRFOIL SECTION USA 35 B

AILERON SPAR BRACE (BETWEEN RIBS)

CONTROL HORN STOPS

AILERON PIVOT

WING RIB AT AILERON CONTROL HORN SCALE X2
WOODEN SPAR WING WITH FRISE AILERONS

WIRE BRACE

FIN POST

2-PIECE CENTRAL ELEVATOR HORN

DISTANCE PIECE

FUSELAGE UPPER LONGERON

SCREW JACK

TAILPLANE YOKE

TAILPLANE PIVOT

TAILPLANE

JOCKEY PULLEY

ELEVATOR

SCALE X 2

TRIM CABLES

TAILWHEEL STEERING HORN (OPTIONAL)

RUDDER HORN

ELEVATOR CONTROL CABLE

WING ATTACHMENT POINTS

OIL TANK FILLER

WIRE BRACING WELDED TO TUBE

ELEVATOR HORN

TAILPLANE PIVOT BRACKET

SCRAP VIEW ABOVE OF TAILPLANE AND ELEVATOR CONTROLS

FAIRING STRUCTURE

ALL ENGINE DETAILS PAINTED BLACK

CRANKCASE BREATHER

EXHAUST PIPE

AIR HEATER SHROUD

HEATER AIR INTAKE

CARB HEAT AIR SUPPLY

CABIN HEATER AND VENTILATOR

¼" CHANNEL SECTION STEEL FAIRING STRUCTURE (EARLIER MODELS USED WOODEN STRIPS)

WELDED STEEL TUBE FRAME

GUIDES FOR SLIDING WINDOW (PORT ONLY)

▲ STBD SIDE ONLY
DOTTED MEMBERS PORT SIDE ONLY

OIL TANK

INSTALLATION OF CONTINENTAL A65

CARBURETTOR INTAKE & FILTER

OIL TANK

EXHAUST MANIFOLDS OMITTED ON THESE VIEWS

EXTENT OF ALUM SHEET NOSE CAPPING — UPPER LOWER

ASH TIP BOW

INTERNAL AILERON CABLE & PULLEY

EXTERNAL AILERON CABLE & PULLEYS

UNDERSIDE OF PORT WING FRAME WOODEN SPARS FRISE AILERONS

¼" CHANNEL STIFFENERS

▲ **Scrap views**
*Fuselage structure and engine details*

# Macchi C200 Saetta

**Country of origin:** Italy.
**Type:** Single-seat, land-based fighter.
**Dimensions:** Wing span 34ft 8½in *10.58m*; length 26ft 10½in *8.20m*; height 11ft 6in *3.51m*; wing area 180.8 sq ft *16.8m²*.
**Weights:** Empty 3903lb *1770kg*; loaded

4851lb *2200kg*.
**Powerplant:** One Fiat A74 RC.38 radial engine rated at 840hp.
**Performance:** Maximum speed 303mph *488kph* at 15,000ft *4570m*; time to 3280ft *1000m*, 1.05min; service ceiling 33,000ft *10,060m*; range (normal) 354 miles

*570km*.
**Armament:** Two fixed 12.7mm Breda-SAFAT machine guns, plus (late models) two fixed 7.7mm machine guns.
**Service:** First flight (prototype) 24 December 1937; service entry autumn 1939.

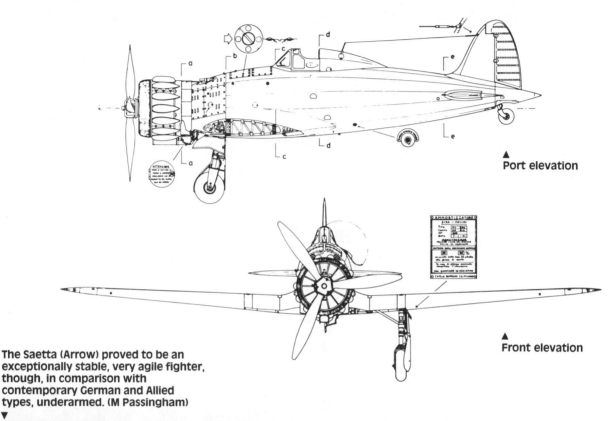

▲ Port elevation

▲ Front elevation

The Saetta (Arrow) proved to be an exceptionally stable, very agile fighter, though, in comparison with contemporary German and Allied types, underarmed. (M Passingham)
▼

The C200's early enclosed canopy was disliked by Italian pilots and eventually discarded in favour of a semi-open cockpit, as here. (M Passingham)

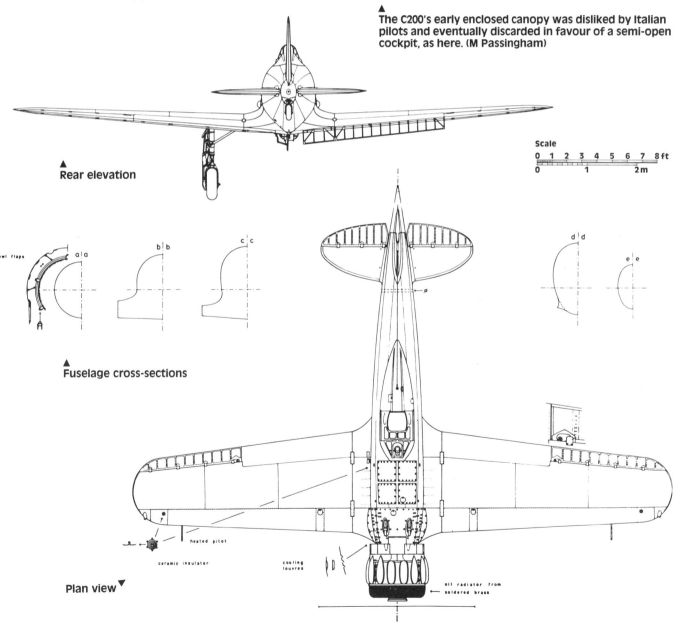

▲ Rear elevation

**Scale**
0 1 2 3 4 5 6 7 8 ft
0 1 2 m

cowl flaps

▲ Fuselage cross-sections

heated pitot

ceramic insulator

cooling louvres

oil radiator from soldered brass

Plan view ▼

Underplan
▼

flaps hydr. actuator

W – W

A – A

▲ Wing cross-sections

W

W

W

A

A

DEFLECTIONS

| | |
|---|---|
| ±25° | Elevator |
| ±30° | Rudder |
| ±25° | Ailerons |
| 45° | |
| +1.45° / –5.30° | Stab |

Aer. Macchi
C.200
P.V.-kg.1960
C.U.-kg. 519

M.M.7705

Starbord elevation

Late-production Saetta in pristine, factory finish of dark
green and light grey, with yellow cowling and white
fuselage band. (Pilot Press)

C.G.

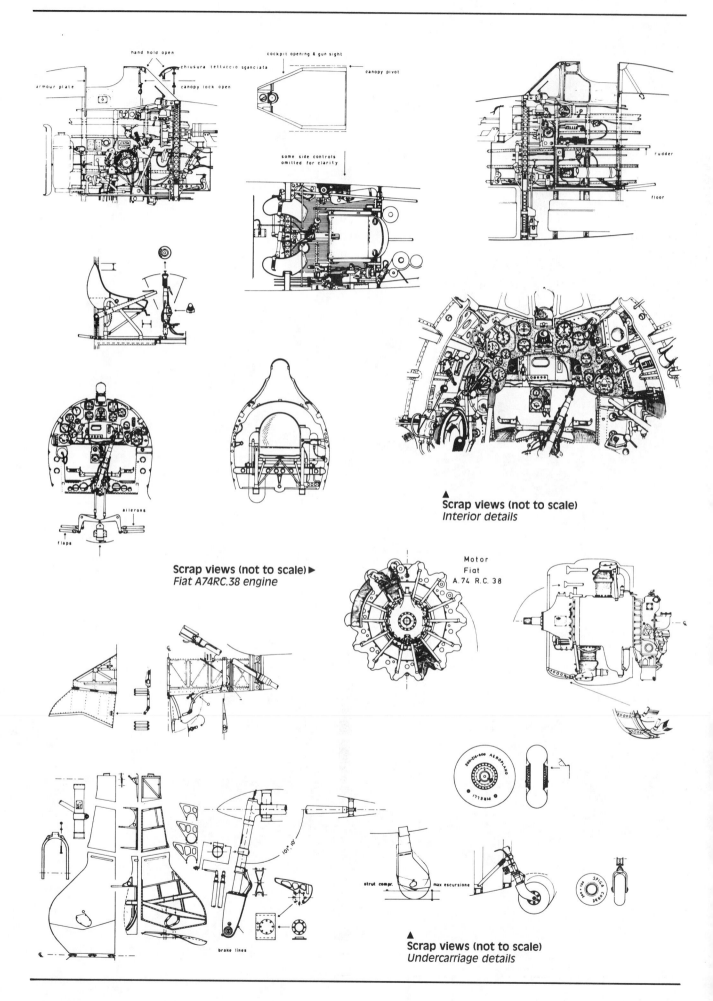

hand hold open

chiusura tettuccio sganciata

canopy lock open

armour plate

cockpit opening & gun sight

canopy pivot

some side controls omitted for clarity

rudder

floor

**Scrap views (not to scale)**
*Interior details*

ailerons

flaps

**Scrap views (not to scale)** ▶
*Fiat A74RC.38 engine*

Motor
Fiat
A.74 R.C. 38

strut compr.        max escursione

brake lines

**Scrap views (not to scale)**
*Undercarriage details*

# Gregor FDB-1

**Country of origin:** Canada.
**Type:** Single-seat, land-based fighter/dive-bomber.
**Dimensions:** Wing span 28ft 0in *8.53m*; length 22ft 0¼in *6.71m*; wing area 194 sq ft *18.02m²*.
**Weights:** Empty 2280lb *1034kg*; loaded 4100lb *1859kg*.
**Powerplant:** One Pratt & Whitney R-1535-SB4-G Twin Wasp Junior fourteen-cylinder radial engine rated at 750hp.
**Performance:** Maximum speed 261mph *420kph*; initial climb rate 2800ft/min *850m/min*; absolute ceiling 27,700ft *8440m*; range (clean) about 1000 miles *1600km*.
**Armament:** Provision for two fixed 0.50in machine guns, plus two 116lb *53kg* bombs.
**Service:** First flight 3 March 1939.

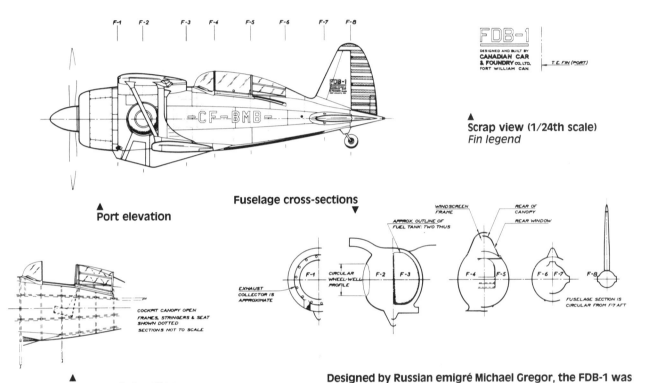

▲ **Port elevation**

**Scrap view (1/24th scale)**
*Fin legend*

**Fuselage cross-sections** ▼

▲ **Scrap port elevation**
*Showing interior detail*

Designed by Russian emigré Michael Gregor, the FDB-1 was rolled out in December 1938 for a series of publicity photos at Fort William, Ontario. Guns would have been installed in the upper wing centre section. (H Robinson) ▼

**Front elevation** ▼

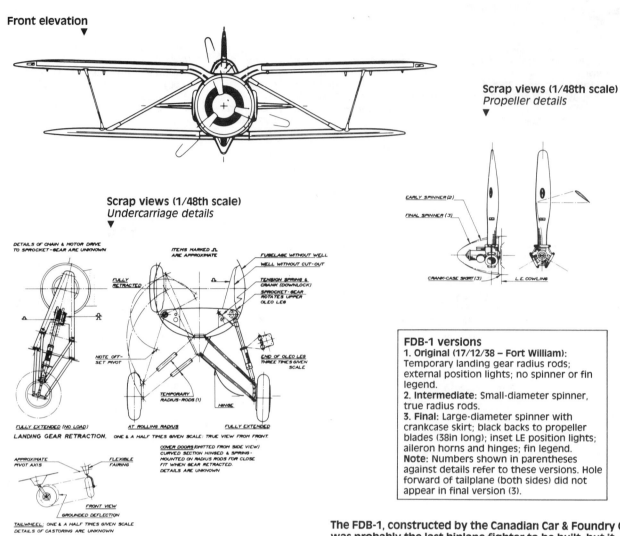

**Scrap views (1/48th scale)**
*Propeller details* ▼

EARLY SPINNER (2)

FINAL SPINNER (3)

CRANK-CASE SKIRT (3)    L.E. COWLING

**Scrap views (1/48th scale)**
*Undercarriage details* ▼

DETAILS OF CHAIN & MOTOR DRIVE
TO SPROCKET-GEAR ARE UNKNOWN

ITEMS MARKED Ω
ARE APPROXIMATE

FUSELAGE WITHOUT WELL

WELL WITHOUT CUT-OUT

FULLY
RETRACTED

TENSION SPRING &
CRANK (DOWNLOCK)
SPROCKET-GEAR
ROTATES UPPER
OLEO LEG

NOTE OFF-
SET PIVOT

END OF OLEO LEG
THREE TIMES GIVEN
SCALE

TEMPORARY
RADIUS-RODS (1)

HINGE

FULLY EXTENDED (NO LOAD)
LANDING GEAR RETRACTION.

AT ROLLING RADIUS
ONE & A HALF TIMES GIVEN SCALE: TRUE VIEW FROM FRONT.

FULLY EXTENDED

APPROXIMATE
PIVOT AXIS

FLEXIBLE
FAIRING

COVER DOORS (OMITTED FROM SIDE VIEW)
CURVED SECTION HINGED & SPRING-
MOUNTED ON RADIUS RODS FOR CLOSE
FIT WHEN GEAR RETRACTED.
DETAILS ARE UNKNOWN

FRONT VIEW
GROUNDED DEFLECTION

TAILWHEEL: ONE & A HALF TIMES GIVEN SCALE
DETAILS OF CASTORING ARE UNKNOWN

---

**FDB-1 versions**
**1. Original (17/12/38 – Fort William):**
Temporary landing gear radius rods;
external position lights; no spinner or fin
legend.
**2. Intermediate:** Small-diameter spinner,
true radius rods.
**3. Final:** Large-diameter spinner with
crankcase skirt; black backs to propeller
blades (38in long); inset LE position lights;
aileron horns and hinges; fin legend.
**Note:** Numbers shown in parentheses
against details refer to these versions. Hole
forward of tailplane (both sides) did not
appear in final version (3).

---

The FDB-1, constructed by the Canadian Car & Foundry Co,
was probably the last biplane fighter to be built, but it
failed to arouse official interest. (H Robinson)
▼

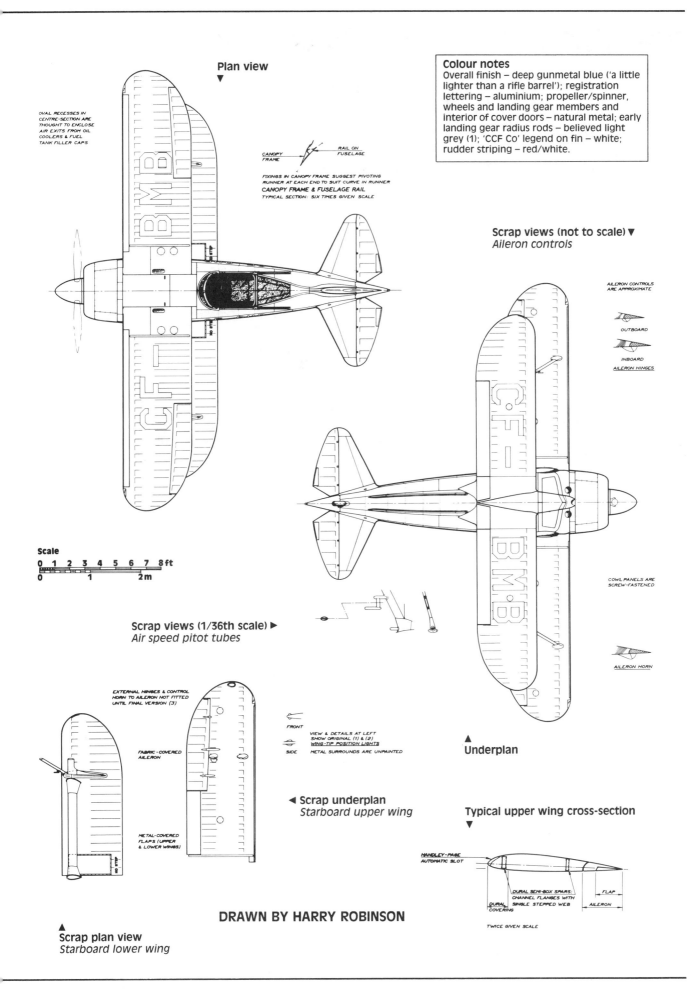

**Plan view**
▼

OVAL RECESSES IN CENTRE-SECTION ARE THOUGHT TO ENCLOSE AIR EXITS FROM OIL COOLERS & FUEL TANK FILLER CAPS

RAIL ON FUSELAGE

CANOPY FRAME

FIXINGS IN CANOPY FRAME SUGGEST PIVOTING RUNNER AT EACH END TO SUIT CURVE IN RUNNER
**CANOPY FRAME & FUSELAGE RAIL**
TYPICAL SECTION: SIX TIMES GIVEN SCALE

**Colour notes**
Overall finish – deep gunmetal blue ('a little lighter than a rifle barrel'); registration lettering – aluminium; propeller/spinner, wheels and landing gear members and interior of cover doors – natural metal; early landing gear radius rods – believed light grey (1); 'CCF Co' legend on fin – white; rudder striping – red/white.

**Scrap views (not to scale)** ▼
*Aileron controls*

AILERON CONTROLS ARE APPROXIMATE

OUTBOARD

INBOARD
*AILERON HINGES*

COWL PANELS ARE SCREW-FASTENED

AILERON HORN

**Scale**

0 1 2 3 4 5 6 7 8 ft

0          1          2m

**Scrap views (1/36th scale)** ►
*Air speed pitot tubes*

**Underplan**
▲

EXTERNAL HINGES & CONTROL HORN TO AILERON NOT FITTED UNTIL FINAL VERSION (3)

FABRIC-COVERED AILERON

METAL-COVERED FLAPS (UPPER & LOWER WINGS)

FRONT

SIDE

VIEW & DETAILS AT LEFT SHOW ORIGINAL (1) & (2)
*WING-TIP POSITION LIGHTS*
METAL SURROUNDS ARE UNPAINTED

◄ **Scrap underplan**
*Starboard upper wing*

**Typical upper wing cross-section**
▼

HANDLEY-PAGE AUTOMATIC SLOT

DURAL SEMI-BOX SPARS: CHANNEL FLANGES WITH SINGLE STEPPED WEB

DURAL COVERING

FLAP

AILERON

TWICE GIVEN SCALE

**DRAWN BY HARRY ROBINSON**

▲
**Scrap plan view**
*Starboard lower wing*

# Douglas SBD-3 and -5 Dauntless

**Country of origin:** USA.
**Type:** Two-seat, carrier-based scout/dive bomber.
**Dimensions:** Wing span 41ft 0in *12.50m*; length 32ft 0in *9.75m*; height 13ft 0in *3.96m*; wing area 325 sq ft *30.19m²*.
**Weights:** Empty 6535lb *2964kg*; loaded 9519lb *4317kg*.
**Powerplant:** One Wright R-1820-52

Cyclone nine-cylinder radial engine rated 1000hp, (-5) R-1820-60 rated at 1200hp.
**Performance:** Maximum speed 255mph *411kph* at 14,000ft *4265m*; time to 10,000ft *3050m*, 7min; service ceiling 25,200ft *7680m*; range (max bomb load) 450 miles *725km*.
**Armament:** One 1000lb *454kg* or 500lb

*227kg* bomb on fuselage cradle and two 100lb *45kg* bombs on wing racks, plus two fixed 0.5in Browning and one or (-5) two flexibly mounted 0.3in machine guns.
**Service:** First flight (XBT-1) July 1935; service entry (SBD-1) 4 June 1940, (-3) December 1940.

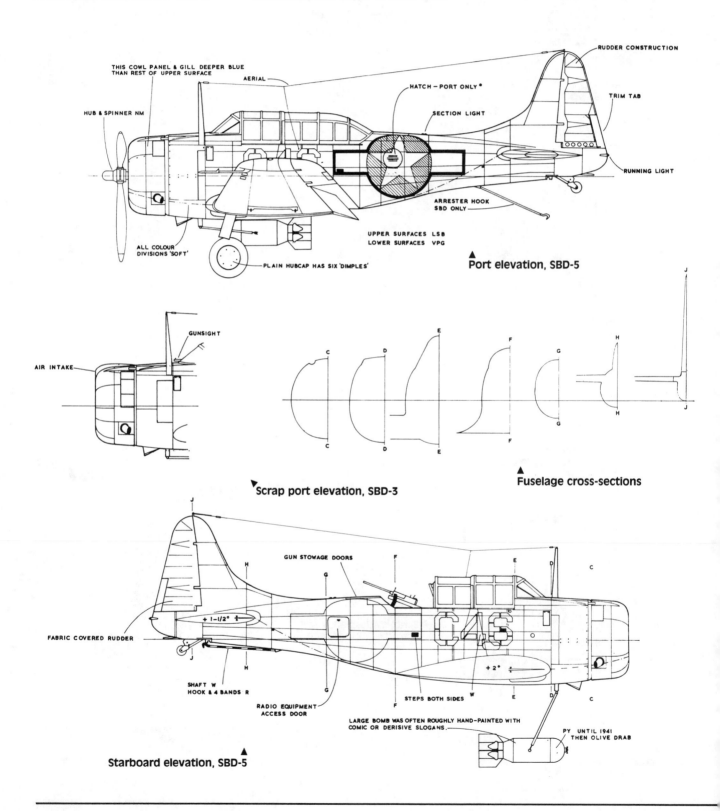

▲ Port elevation, SBD-5

▼ Scrap port elevation, SBD-3

▲ Fuselage cross-sections

▲ Starboard elevation, SBD-5

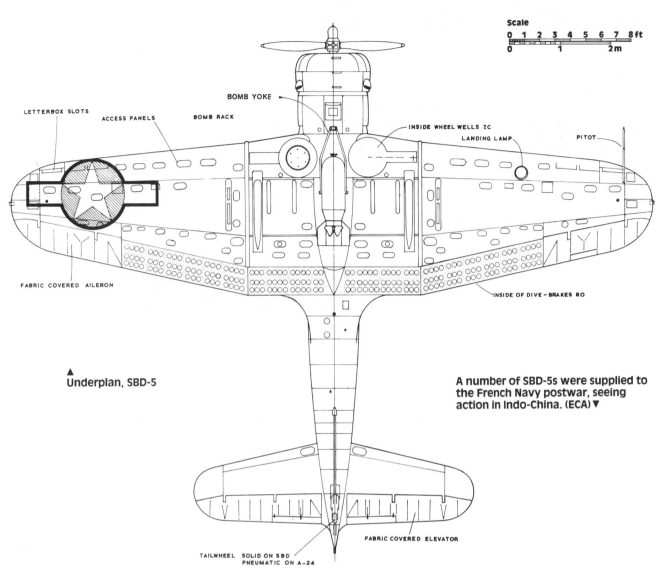

Scale
0 1 2 3 4 5 6 7 8 ft
0 1 2m

BOMB YOKE

LETTERBOX SLOTS

ACCESS PANELS

BOMB RACK

INSIDE WHEEL WELLS ZC

LANDING LAMP

PITOT

FABRIC COVERED AILERON

INSIDE OF DIVE-BRAKES RO

▲
Underplan, SBD-5

**A number of SBD-5s were supplied to the French Navy postwar, seeing action in Indo-China. (ECA)** ▼

TAILWHEEL SOLID ON SBD
PNEUMATIC ON A-24

FABRIC COVERED ELEVATOR

▲ Dauntless in civilian hands in the 1950s, apparently fitted for skywriting. Other ex-military SBDs were used for crop-dusting. (J Gradidge)

Plan view, SBD-5
▼

FLANGE FAIRING

LETTERBOX SLOTS

FORMATION LIGHT

RUNNING LIGHT

AILERON CONSTRUCTION

WING WALK M8

TRIM TAB – PORT ONLY

PERFORATED DIVE–BRAKE

*STENCIL ON HATCH:
LIFE RAFT &
EMERGENCY
RATIONS

A—A

B—B

▲ Wing cross-sections

**Scale**

0 1 2 3 4 5 6 7 8 ft

0      1      2 m

TRIM TAB

ELEVATOR CONSTRUCTION

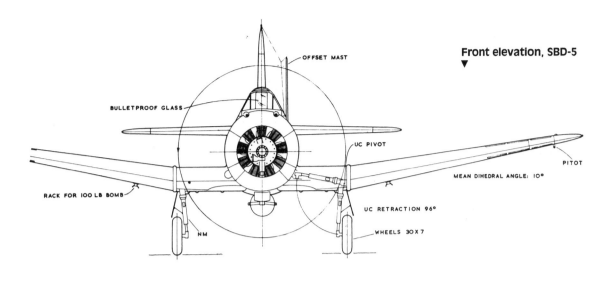

Front elevation, SBD-5
▼

OFFSET MAST

BULLETPROOF GLASS

UC PIVOT

PITOT

MEAN DIHEDRAL ANGLE: 10°

RACK FOR 100 LB BOMB

NM

UC RETRACTION 96°

WHEELS 30 X 7

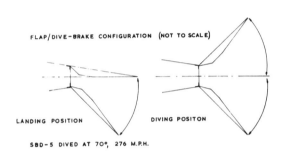

FLAP/DIVE-BRAKE CONFIGURATION (NOT TO SCALE)

LANDING POSITION

DIVING POSITON

SBD-5 DIVED AT 70°, 276 M.P.H.

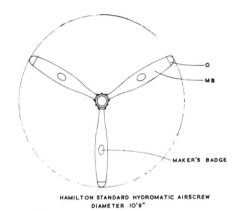

O

MB

MAKER'S BADGE

HAMILTON STANDARD HYDROMATIC AIRSCREW
DIAMETER 10'9"

FREISE-TYPE AILERON DETAIL
(NOT TO SCALE)

◄ **Scrap views (not to scale)**
*Flap/dive brake configuration*

▲
**Propeller details**

## Colour code

LSB – Light smoky blue; **VPG** – Very pale grey;
**RB** – Dirty royal blue; **ZC** – ZC (zinc chromate)
green; **R** – Red; **W** – White; **O** – Orange; **RO** –
Red-orange; **PY** – Pale yellow; **MB** – Matt
black; **IB** – Insignia Blue (Navy); **NM** – Natural
metal.

R
W
IB
RB

① UNTIL 17.8.42

② 18.8.42–29.6.43

③          30.6.43–SEPT. 43

④          SEPT. 43 ON

▲
**Scrap views (not to scale)**
*National insignia*

---

**Summary of external differences,
SBD-5 and SBD-3**

**1.** Air intake on cowl top, SBD-3; absent on
SBD-5.
**2.** Three cowl gills, SBD-3; one on SBD-5.
**3.** External gunsight, SBD-3; absent on
SBD-5.
**4.** Single gun in rear cockpit, SBD-3; twin
guns in SBD-5.

**DRAWN BY D PLATT**

# Focke-Wulf Fw 190A-5, A-9, F and G

**Country of origin:** Germany.
**Type:** Single-seat, land-based fighter and (F, G) fighter-bomber.
**Dimensions:** Wing span 34ft 5½in *10.5m*; length 29ft 0in *8.84m*; height 13ft 0in *3.96m*; wing area 196.98 sq ft *18.3m²*.
**Weights:** Empty 7000lb *3176kg*, (F) 7328lb *3325kg*; normal loaded 9750lb *4424kg*, (F) 9700lb *4401kg*; maximum 10,800lb *4900kg*, (F) 10,850lb *4923kg*.
**Powerplant:** One BMW 801D fourteen-cylinder radial engine rated at 1700hp,

(A-9) 801F rated at 2000hp, (F, G) 801D-2 rated at 1700hp.
**Performance:** Maximum speed (clean) 408mph *657kph* at 20,670ft *6300m*, (F, clean) 394mph *634kph* at 18,050ft *5500m*; initial climb rate 2350ft/min *720m/min*, (F) 2110ft/min *640m/min*; service ceiling 33,800ft *10,300m*, (F) 34,800ft *10,600m*; range (normal) 500 miles *800km*.
**Armament:** Two fixed 20mm MG 151 cannon, two fixed 20mm MG FF cannon and two fixed 7.9mm MG 17 machine

guns, (A-9) four fixed 20mm MG 151 cannon and two fixed 13mm MG 131 machine guns, (F) two fixed 20mm MG 151 cannon and two fixed 7.9mm MG 17 machine guns plus one 550lb *250kg* bomb, (G) two fixed 20mm MG 151 cannon plus one 1100lb *500kg*, 2200 *1000kg* or 3960lb *1800kg* bomb.
**Service:** First flight (Fw 190V-1) 1 June 1939, (F) late 1942; service entry (A-5) summer 1943, (G) autumn 1943.

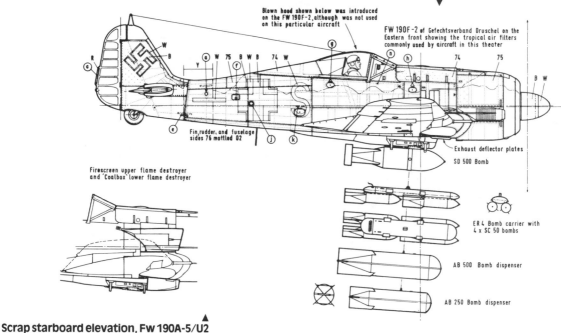

Scrap starboard elevation, Fw 190A-5/U2
*Wk Nr 1083, Ge+LA*

Starboard elevation, Fw 190F-2

Port elevation, Fw 190A-5

Scale

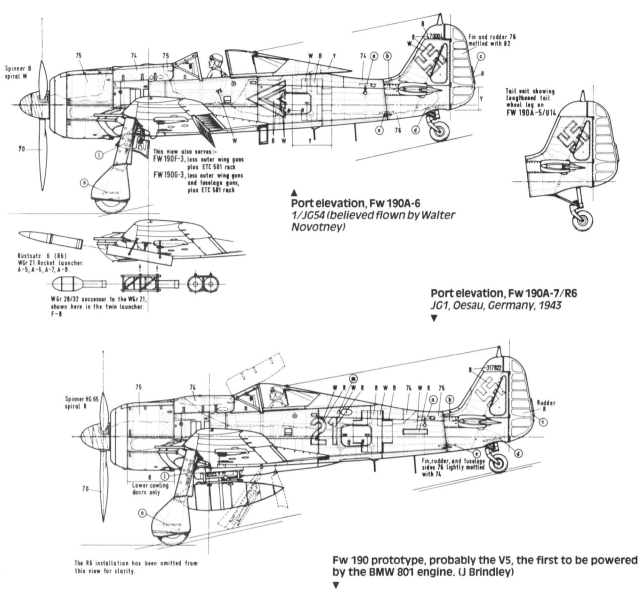

Spinner B
spiral W

75    74    75

70

This view also serves:-
FW 190 F-3, less outer wing guns
plus ETC 501 rack

FW 190 G-3, less outer wing guns
and fuselage guns,
plus ETC 501 rack

Rüstsatz 6 (R6)
WGr 21 Rocket launcher.
A-5, A-6, A-7, A-8.

WGr 28/32 successor to the WGr 21,
shown here in the twin launcher.
F-8

W B Y

74    (a)    (b)

(c)

(e)    76    (d)

B  W    Y

B    470004

W

Fin and rudder 76
mottled with 02

R

Y

Tail unit showing
lengthened tail
wheel leg on
FW 190A-5/U14

**Port elevation, Fw 190A-6**
*1/JG54 (believed flown by Walter
Novotney)*

**Port elevation, Fw 190A-7/R6**
*JG1, Oesau, Germany, 1943*
▼

Spinner HG 65
spiral R

75    74

70

Lower cowling
doors only

R    (l)

The R6 installation has been omitted from
this view for clarity.

W R W R    B W B    74  W  R    75

B    317822

(a)    (b)

(c)

(d)

Rudder
R

Fin, rudder, and fuselage
sides 76 lightly mottled
with 74

**Fw 190 prototype, probably the V5, the first to be powered
by the BMW 801 engine. (J Brindley)**
▼

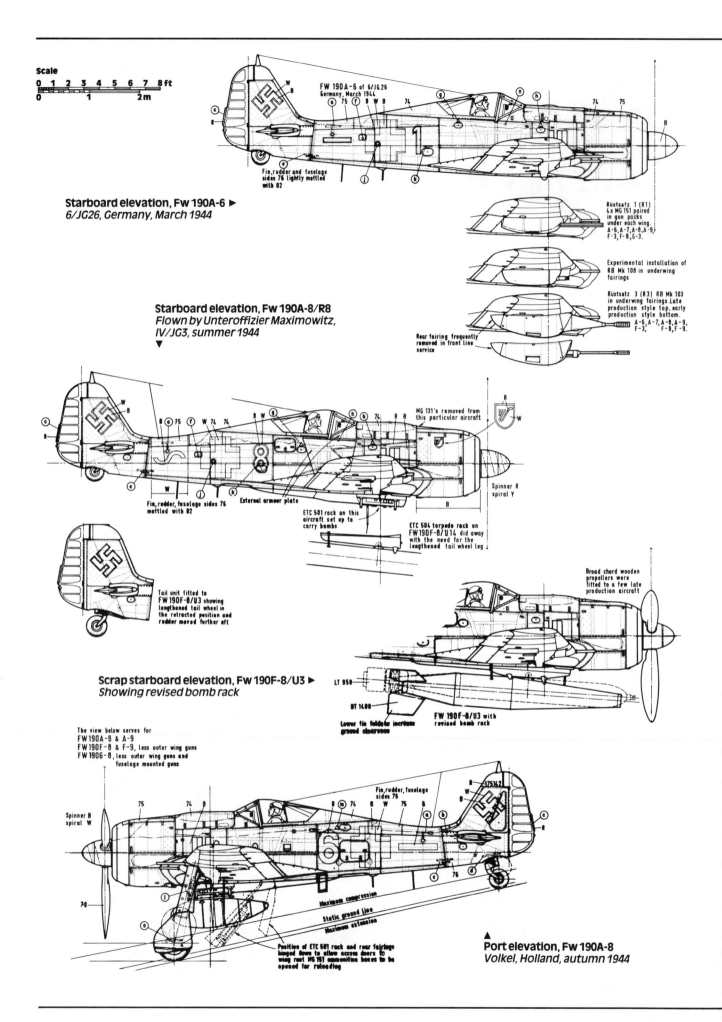

**Scale**

0 1 2 3 4 5 6 7 8 ft

0      1      2 m

FW 190A-6 of 6/JG.26
Germany, March 1944

**Starboard elevation, Fw 190A-6 ▶**
*6/JG26, Germany, March 1944*

Fin, rudder and fuselage
sides 76 lightly mottled
with 02

Rüstsatz 1 (R1)
4 x MG 151 paired
in gun packs
under each wing.
A-6, A-7, A-8, A-9,
F-3, F-8, G-3.

Experimental installation of
RB Mk 108 in underwing
fairings

Rüstsatz 3 (R3) RB Mk 103
in underwing fairings. Late
production style top, early
production style bottom.
A-6, A-7, A-8, A-9,
F-3,    F-8, F-9.

Rear fairing frequently
removed in front line
service

**Starboard elevation, Fw 190A-8/R8**
*Flown by Unteroffizier Maximowitz,
IV/JG3, summer 1944*
▼

MG 131's removed from
this particular aircraft

Fin, rudder, fuselage sides 76
mottled with 02

External armour plate

ETC 501 rack on this
aircraft set up to
carry bombs

Spinner R
spiral Y

ETC 504 torpedo rack on
FW 190F-8/U14 did away
with the need for the
lengthened tail wheel leg

Tail unit fitted to
FW 190F-8/U3 showing
lengthened tail wheel in
the retracted position and
rudder moved further aft

Broad chord wooden
propellers were
fitted to a few late
production aircraft

**Scrap starboard elevation, Fw 190F-8/U3 ▶**
*Showing revised bomb rack*

LT 950

BT 1400

Lower fin folded to increase
ground clearance

FW 190F-8/U3 with
revised bomb rack

The view below serves for
FW 190A-8 & A-9
FW 190F-8 & F-9, less outer wing guns
FW 190G-8, less outer wing guns and
     fuselage mounted guns

Spinner B
spiral W

Fin, rudder, fuselage
sides 76

Maximum compression

Static ground line

Maximum extension

Position of ETC 501 rack and rear fairings
hinged down to allow access doors to
wing root MG 151 ammunition boxes to be
opened for reloading

**▲ Port elevation, Fw 190A-8**
*Volkel, Holland, autumn 1944*

**DRAWN BY A L BENTLEY**

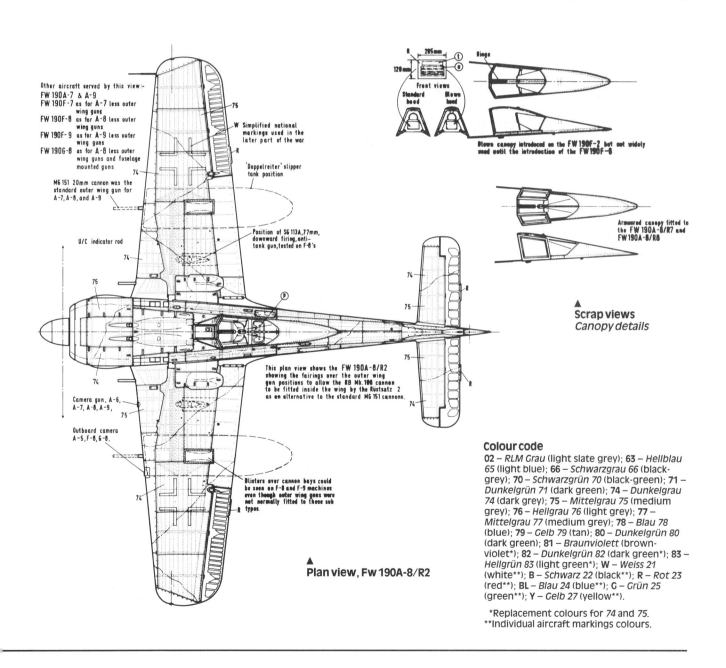

Other aircraft served by this view:-
FW 190A-7 & A-9
FW 190F-7 as for A-7 less outer wing guns
FW 190F-8 as for A-8 less outer wing guns
FW 190F-9 as for A-9 less outer wing guns
FW 190G-8 as for A-8 less outer wing guns and fuselage mounted guns

MG 151 20mm cannon was the standard outer wing gun for A-7, A-8, and A-9

U/C indicator rod

Camera gun, A-6, A-7, A-8, A-9,

Outboard camera A-5, F-8, G-8.

W Simplified national markings used in the later part of the war

'Doppelreiter' slipper tank position

Position of SG 113A,77mm, downward firing, anti-tank gun, tested on F-8's

This plan view shows the FW 190A-8/R2 showing the fairings over the outer wing gun positions to allow the RB Mk.100 cannon to be fitted inside the wing by the Rüstsatz 2 as an alternative to the standard MG 151 cannons.

Blisters over cannon bays could be seen on F-8 and F-9 machines even though outer wing guns were not normally fitted to these sub types.

**Plan view, Fw 190A-8/R2**

Front views
Standard hood     Blown hood

Blown canopy introduced on the FW 190F-2 but not widely used until the introduction of the FW 190F-8

Armoured canopy fitted to the FW 190A-6/R7 and FW 190A-8/R8

**Scrap views**
*Canopy details*

**Colour code**
02 – *RLM Grau* (light slate grey); 63 – *Hellblau 65* (light blue); 66 – *Schwarzgrau 66* (black-grey); 70 – *Schwarzgrün 70* (black-green); 71 – *Dunkelgrün 71* (dark green); 74 – *Dunkelgrau 74* (dark grey); 75 – *Mittelgrau 75* (medium grey); 76 – *Hellgrau 76* (light grey); 77 – *Mittelgrau 77* (medium grey); 78 – *Blau 78* (blue); 79 – *Gelb 79* (tan); 80 – *Dunkelgrün 80* (dark green); 81 – *Braunviolett* (brown-violet*); 82 – *Dunkelgrün 82* (dark green*); 83 – *Hellgrün 83* (light green*); **W** – *Weiss 21* (white**); **B** – *Schwarz 22* (black**); **R** – *Rot 23* (red**); **BL** – *Blau 24* (blue**); **G** – *Grün 25* (green**); **Y** – *Gelb 27* (yellow**).

*Replacement colours for 74 and 75.
**Individual aircraft markings colours.

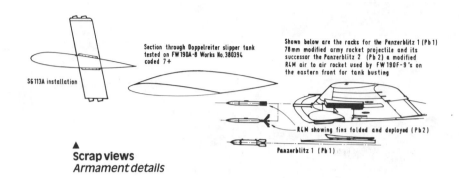

SG 113A installation

Section through Doppelreiter slipper tank tested on FW 190A-8 Works No.380394 coded 7+

Shown below are the racks for the Panzerblitz 1 (Pb 1) 78mm modified army rocket projectile and its successor the Panzerblitz 2 (Pb 2) a modified R4M air to air rocket used by FW 190F-9's on the eastern front for tank busting

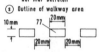

R4M showing fins folded and deployed (Pb 2)

Panzerblitz 1 (Pb 1)

▲ **Scrap views**
*Armament details*

## Scrap views, Fw 190A-5/U4
*Probable layout (two 12.5/7×9 cameras in rear fuselage)*
▼

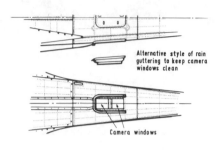

Alternative style of rain guttering to keep camera windows clean

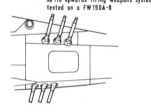

Camera windows

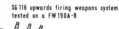

SG 116 upwards firing weapons system tested on a FW 190A-8

(a) (25mm lettering, B)
Hier aufbocken

(b) (20mm lettering, B)
↳ Anzeigegerät O

(c) (20mm lettering, W)
Nicht verstellen

(d) (25mm lettering, B)
Reifendruck 5 atü

(e) (25mm lettering, B)
Hier aufbocken

(f) W
R

(g) W
Y
B — 292 ltr   100mm

(h) W
Y
B — 232 ltr   100mm

(i)

(j)

(k) (5mm lettering, W)
O Sauerstoff O    O

(l) (25mm lettering, B) Stbd leg
Federbein Solldruck
70 64 54 48 40 35 32 über 4600 kg
58 53 44 38 34 30 27 bis 4600 kg

Port leg
Federbein Solldruck
über 4600kg 32 35 40 48 54 64 70
bis 4600kg 27 30 34 38 44 53 58

Alternatives :- Stbd leg
(20mm & 10mm lettering, B)
Federbeindruck

Port leg
(20mm & 10mm lettering, B)
Federbeindruck

(m) W
Y
B — 115 ltr   100mm

(n) (20mm lettering, B)
Haube
↑Auf○Zu↓
drücken

(o) (25mm lettering, B)
Reifendruck 5,5 atü

(p) (25mm lettering,W)
Gepäckraum

(q) (25mm lettering,B)
Hier aufbocken

(r) (75mm lettering, 77)
Nur hier betreten

(s) Outline of walkway area

10mm    77   20mm
20mm    20mm

(t) (25mm lettering, W)
ACHTUNG !

(u) (15mm lettering, W)
Haubenabwurf durch Sprengladung

▲ **Stencilled instructions**
*See main drawings for location*

**Fw 190As stand ready at a Channel coast airfield. The unit appears to be either *JG2* or *JG26*. (J Brindley)**
▼

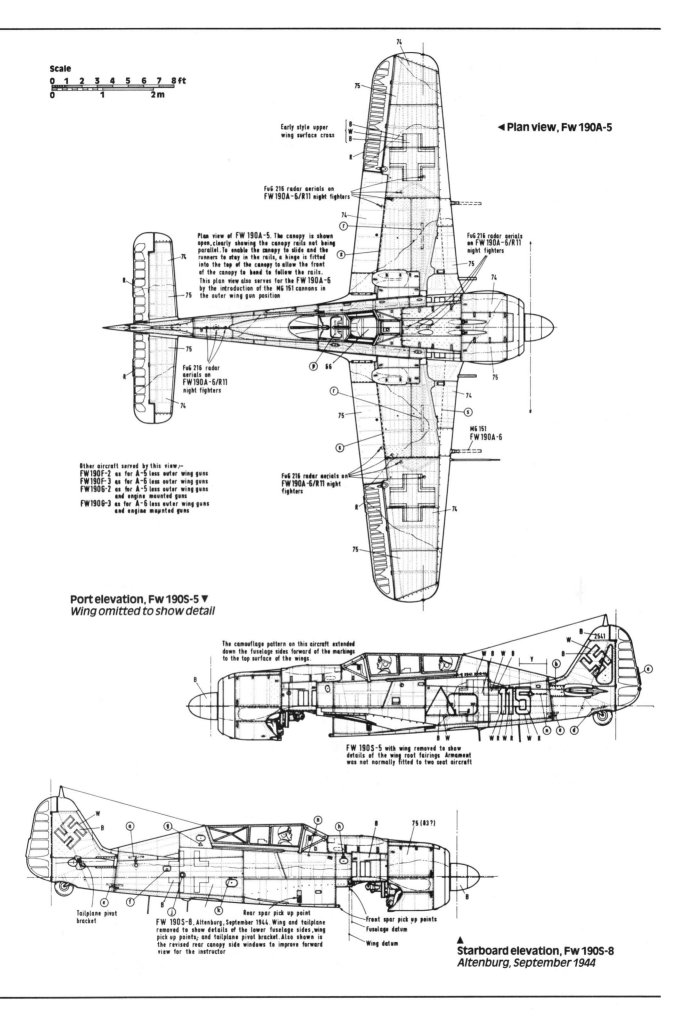

**Scale**

0 1 2 3 4 5 6 7 8 ft

0  1  2m

Early style upper
wing surface cross

◄ **Plan view, Fw 190A-5**

FuG 216 radar aerials on
FW 190A-6/R11 night fighters

Plan view of FW 190A-5. The canopy is shown
open, clearly showing the canopy rails not being
parallel. To enable the canopy to slide and the
runners to stay in the rails, a hinge is fitted
into the top of the canopy to allow the front
of the canopy to bend to follow the rails.
This plan view also serves for the FW 190A-6
by the introduction of the MG 151 cannons in
the outer wing gun position

FuG 216 radar aerials
on FW 190A-6/R11 night
fighters

FuG 216 radar
aerials on
FW 190A-6/R11
night fighters

Other aircraft served by this view:-
FW190F-2 as for A-5 less outer wing guns
FW190F-3 as for A-6 less outer wing guns
FW190G-2 as for A-5 less outer wing guns
and engine mounted guns
FW190G-3 as for A-6 less outer wing guns
and engine mounted guns

MG 151
FW 190A-6

FuG 216 radar aerials on
FW 190A-6/R11 night
fighters

**Port elevation, Fw 190S-5** ▼
*Wing omitted to show detail*

The camouflage pattern on this aircraft extended
down the fuselage sides forward of the markings
to the top surface of the wings.

FW 190S-5 with wing removed to show
details of the wing root fairings Armament
was not normally fitted to two seat aircraft

Tailplane pivot
bracket

Rear spar pick up point

FW 190S-8, Altenburg, September 1944. Wing and tailplane
removed to show details of the lower fuselage sides, wing
pick up points, and tailplane pivot bracket. Also shown is
the revised rear canopy side windows to improve forward
view for the instructor

Front spar pick up points
Fuselage datum
Wing datum

75 (83?)

▲ **Starboard elevation, Fw 190S-8**
*Altenburg, September 1944*

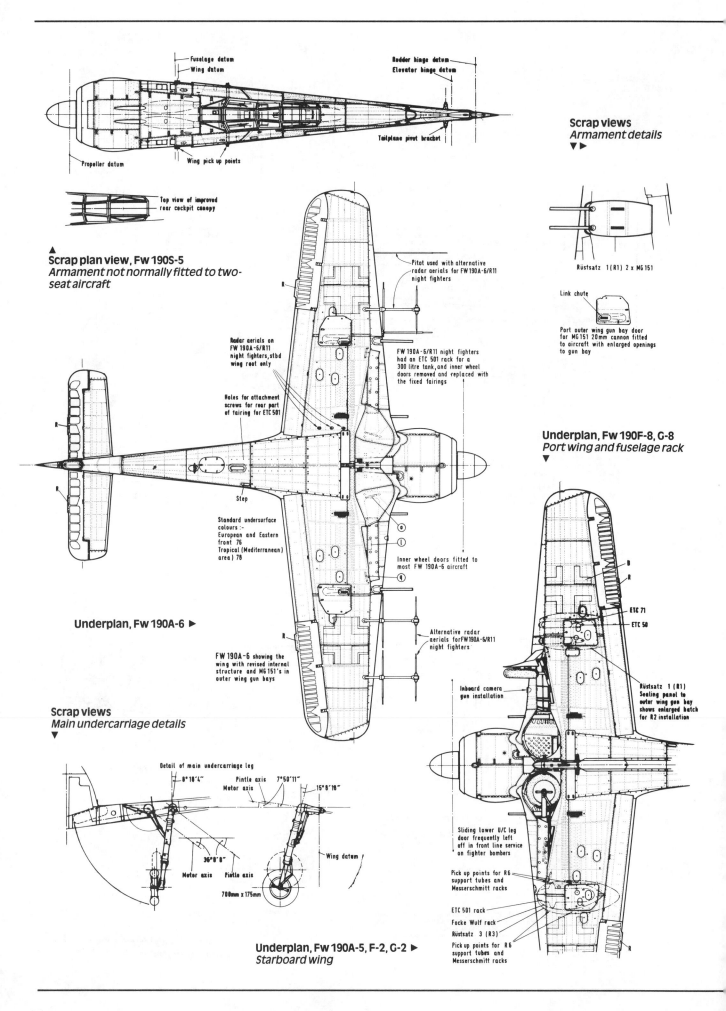

Fuselage datum
Wing datum

Rudder hinge datum
Elevator hinge datum

Propeller datum

Wing pick up points

Tailplane pivot bracket

Top view of improved
rear cockpit canopy

**Scrap plan view, Fw 190S-5**
*Armament not normally fitted to two-seat aircraft*

**Scrap views**
*Armament details*
▼ ►

Rüstsatz 1(R1) 2 x MG 151

Link chute

Port outer wing gun bay door
for MG 151 20mm cannon fitted
to aircraft with enlarged openings
to gun bay

Pitot used with alternative
radar aerials for FW 190A-6/R11
night fighters

Radar aerials on
FW 190A-6/R11
night fighters, stbd
wing root only

FW 190A-6/R11 night fighters
had an ETC 501 rack for a
300 litre tank, and inner wheel
doors removed and replaced with
the fixed fairings

Holes for attachment
screws for rear part
of fairing for ETC 501

**Underplan, Fw 190F-8, G-8**
*Port wing and fuselage rack*
▼

Step

Standard undersurface
colours :-
European and Eastern
front 76
Tropical (Mediterranean)
area) 78

**Underplan, Fw 190A-6** ►

FW 190A-6 showing the
wing with revised internal
structure and MG 151's in
outer wing gun bays

Inner wheel doors fitted to
most FW 190A-6 aircraft

Alternative radar
aerials for FW 190A-6/R11
night fighters

Inboard camera
gun installation

ETC 71
ETC 50

Rüstsatz 1 (R1)
Sealing panel to
outer wing gun bay
shows enlarged hatch
for R2 installation

Sliding lower U/C leg
door frequently left
off in front line service
on fighter bombers

Pick up points for R6
support tubes and
Messerschmitt racks

ETC 501 rack
Focke Wulf rack
Rüstsatz 3 (R3)
Pick up points for R6
support tubes and
Messerschmitt racks

**Scrap views**
*Main undercarriage details*
▼

Detail of main undercarriage leg

0° 18' 4"
Pintle axis
Motor axis

7°50'11"

15° 8' 10"

36°0'0"

Motor axis

Pintle axis

Wing datum

700mm x 175mm

**Underplan, Fw 190A-5, F-2, G-2** ►
*Starboard wing*

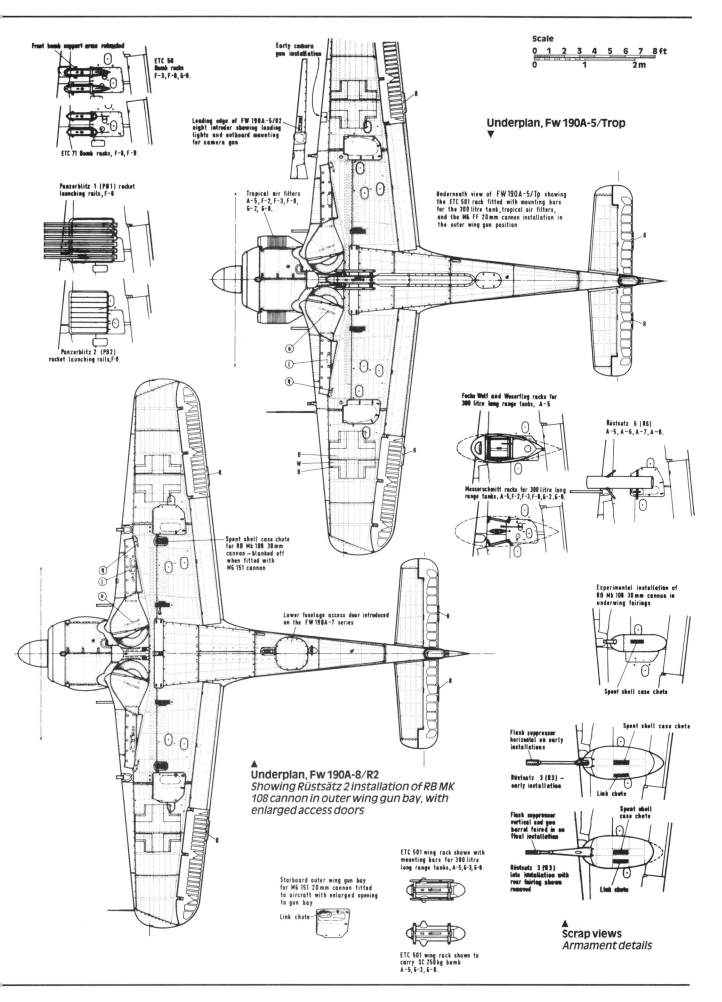

Front bomb support arms retracted

ETC 50 Bomb racks F-3, F-8, G-8.

ETC 71 Bomb racks, F-8, F-9.

Panzerblitz 1 (PB1) rocket launching rails, F-8

Panzerblitz 2 (PB2) rocket launching rails, F-8.

Early camera gun installation

Leading edge of FW 190A-5/U2 night intruder showing landing lights and outboard mounting for camera gun

Tropical air filters A-5, F-2, F-3, F-8, G-2, G-8.

**Underplan, Fw 190A-5/Trop** ▼

Underneath view of FW 190A-5/Tp showing the ETC 501 rack fitted with mounting bars for the 300 litre tank, tropical air filters, and the MG FF 20mm cannon installation in the outer wing gun position

Focke Wulf and Weserflug racks for 300 litre long range tanks, A-5

Messerschmitt racks for 300 litre long range tanks, A-5,F-2,F-3,F-8,G-2,G-8.

Rüstsatz 6 (R6) A-5, A-6, A-7, A-8.

Spent shell case chute for RB Mk 108 30mm cannon — blanked off when fitted with MG 151 cannon

Lower fuselage access door introduced on the FW 190A-7 series

Experimental installation of RB Mk 108 30mm cannon in underwing fairings

Spent shell case chute

▲ **Underplan, Fw 190A-8/R2**
*Showing Rüstsätz 2 installation of RB MK 108 cannon in outer wing gun bay, with enlarged access doors*

Starboard outer wing gun bay for MG 151 20mm cannon fitted to aircraft with enlarged opening to gun bay

Link chute

ETC 501 wing rack shown with mounting bars for 300 litre long range tanks, A-5,6-3, 6-8.

ETC 501 wing rack shown to carry SC 250kg bomb A-5, 6-3, 6-8.

Flash suppresser horizontal on early installations

Rüstsatz 3 (R3) — early installation

Link chute

Spent shell case chute

Flash suppresser vertical and gun barrel faired in on final installation

Rüstsatz 3 (R3) late installation with rear fairing shown removed

Spent shell case chute

Link chute

▲ **Scrap views**
*Armament details*

Scale
0 1 2 3 4 5 6 7 8 ft
0 1 2m

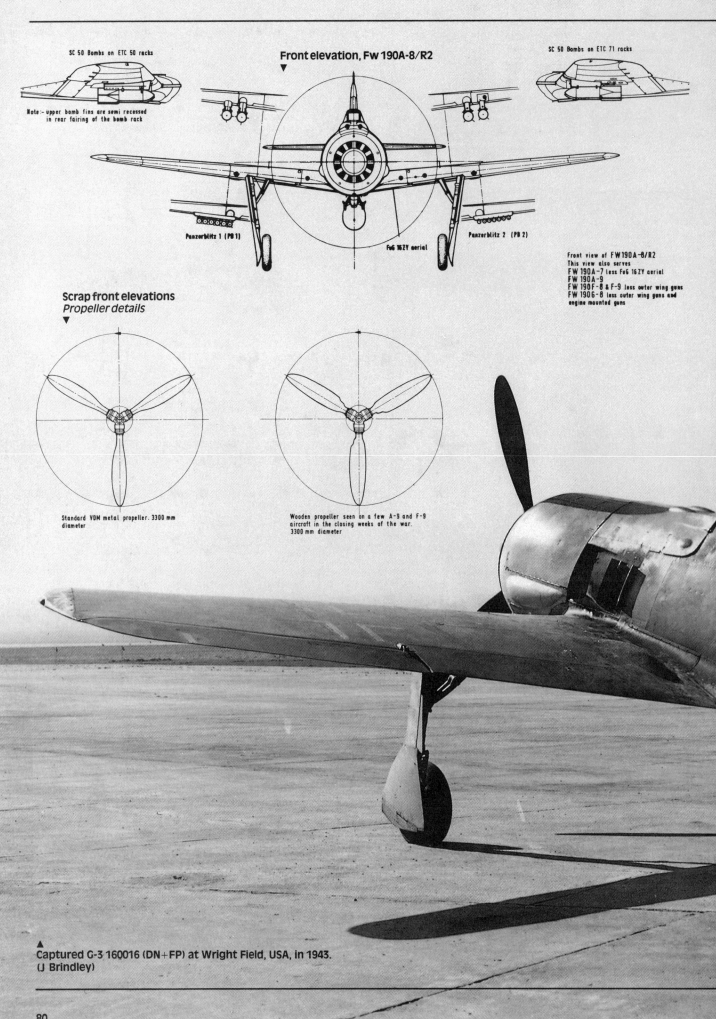

SC 50 Bombs on ETC 50 racks

Note:- upper bomb fins are semi recessed in rear fairing of the bomb rack

**Front elevation, Fw 190A-8/R2**
▼

SC 50 Bombs on ETC 71 racks

Panzerblitz 1 (PB 1)

Panzerblitz 2 (PB 2)

FuG 16ZY aerial

Front view of FW 190A-8/R2
This view also serves
FW 190A-7 less FuG 16ZY aerial
FW 190A-9
FW 190F-8 & F-9 less outer wing guns
FW 190G-8 less outer wing guns and
engine mounted guns

## Scrap front elevations
*Propeller details*
▼

Standard VDM metal propeller. 3300 mm diameter

Wooden propeller seen on a few A-9 and F-9 aircraft in the closing weeks of the war. 3300 mm diameter

▲
**Captured G-3 160016 (DN+FP) at Wright Field, USA, in 1943.**
**(J Brindley)**

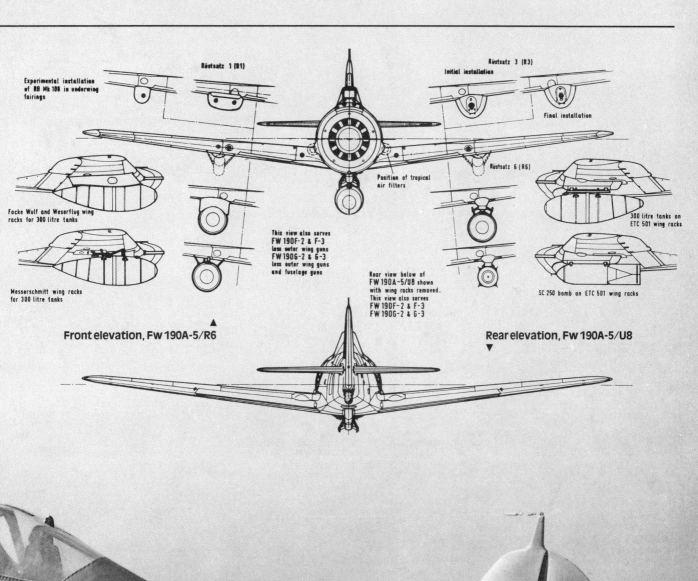

Experimental installation of R8 Mk 108 in underwing fairings

Rüstsatz 1 (R1)

Rüstsatz 3 (R3)
Initial installation

Final installation

Position of tropical air filters

Rüstsatz 6 (R6)

Focke Wulf and Weserflug wing racks for 300 litre tanks

Messerschmitt wing racks for 300 litre tanks

This view also serves FW 190F-2 & F-3 less outer wing guns FW 190G-2 & G-3 less outer wing guns and fuselage guns

300 litre tanks on ETC 501 wing racks

SC 250 bomb on ETC 501 wing racks

**Front elevation, Fw 190A-5/R6** ▲

Rear view below of FW 190A-5/U8 shown with wing racks removed. This view also serves FW 190F-2 & F-3 FW 190G-2 & G-3

**Rear elevation, Fw 190A-5/U8** ▼

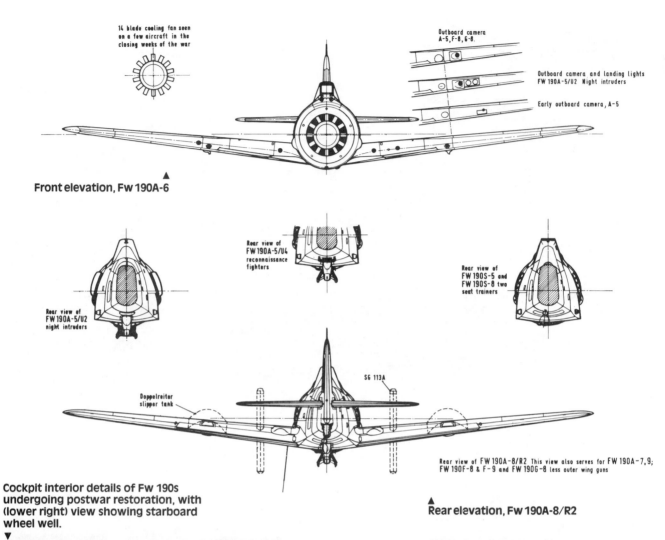

14 blade cooling fan seen on a few aircraft in the closing weeks of the war

Outboard camera A-5, F-8, G-8.

Outboard camera and landing lights FW 190A-5/U2 Night intruders

Early outboard camera, A-5

**Front elevation, Fw 190A-6** ▲

Rear view of FW 190A-5/U4 reconnaissance fighters

Rear view of FW 190A-5/U2 night intruders

Rear view of FW 190S-5 and FW 190S-8 two seat trainers

SG 113A

Doppelreiter slipper tank

Rear view of FW 190A-8/R2 This view also serves for FW 190A-7, 9; FW 190F-8 & F-9 and FW 190G-8 less outer wing guns

**Rear elevation, Fw 190A-8/R2** ▲

**Cockpit interior details of Fw 190s undergoing postwar restoration, with (lower right) view showing starboard wheel well.**
▼

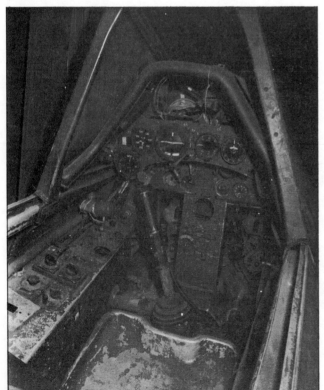

▲
**Fw 190A-4 GL+MY with underbelly rack and, typically, mottled paintwork on fuselage sides and denser colouring on upper surfaces. (RAF Museum)**

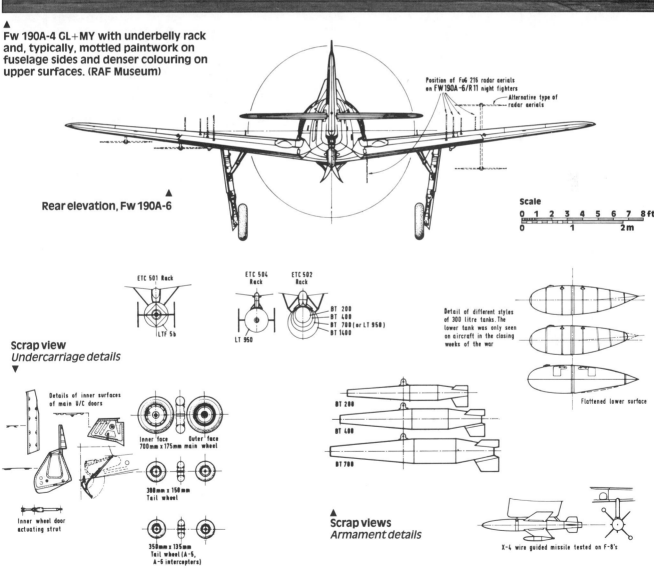

Position of FuG 216 radar aerials on FW 190A-6/R 11 night fighters

Alternative type of radar aerials

▲
**Rear elevation, Fw 190A-6**

Scale

0 1 2 3 4 5 6 7 8 ft

0 1 2m

ETC 501 Rack

LTF 5b

ETC 504 Rack

LT 950

ETC 502 Rack

BT 200
BT 400
BT 700 (or LT 950)
BT 1400

Detail of different styles of 300 litre tanks. The lower tank was only seen on aircraft in the closing weeks of the war

Flattened lower surface

**Scrap view**
*Undercarriage details*
▼

Details of inner surfaces of main U/C doors

Inner face    Outer face
700mm x 175mm main wheel

300mm x 150mm Tail wheel

Inner wheel door actuating strut

350mm x 135mm Tail wheel (A-5, A-6 interceptors)

BT 200

BT 400

BT 700

**Scrap views**
*Armament details*

X-4 wire guided missile tested on F-8's

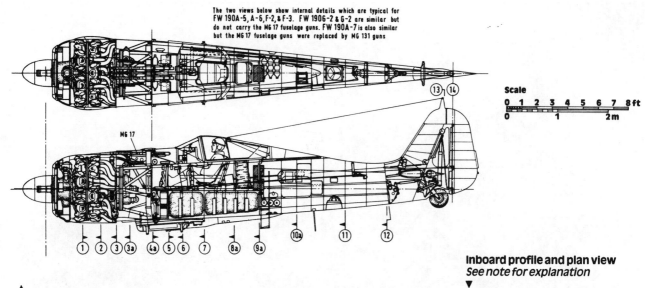

The two views below show internal details which are typical for
FW 190A-5, A-6, F-2, & F-3. FW 190G-2 & G-2 are similar but
do not carry the MG 17 fuselage guns. FW 190A-7 is also similar
but the MG 17 fuselage guns were replaced by MG 131 guns

MG 17

**Inboard profile and plan view**
*See note for explanation*
▲

**Inboard profile and plan view**
*See note for explanation*
▼

Scale
0 1 2 3 4 5 6 7 8 ft
0 1 2m

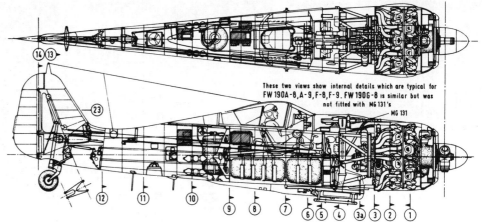

These two views show internal details which are typical for
FW 190A-8, A-9, F-8, F-9. FW 190G-8 is similar but was
not fitted with MG 131's

MG 131

**Fuselage cross-sections**
▼

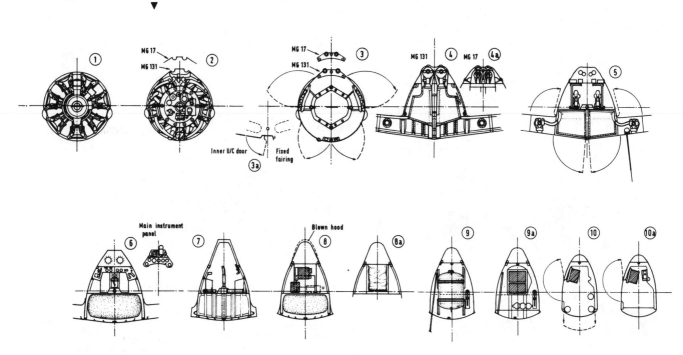

MG 17
MG 131

MG 17
MG 131

MG 131    MG 17

Inner U/C door    Fixed fairing

Main instrument panel

Blown hood

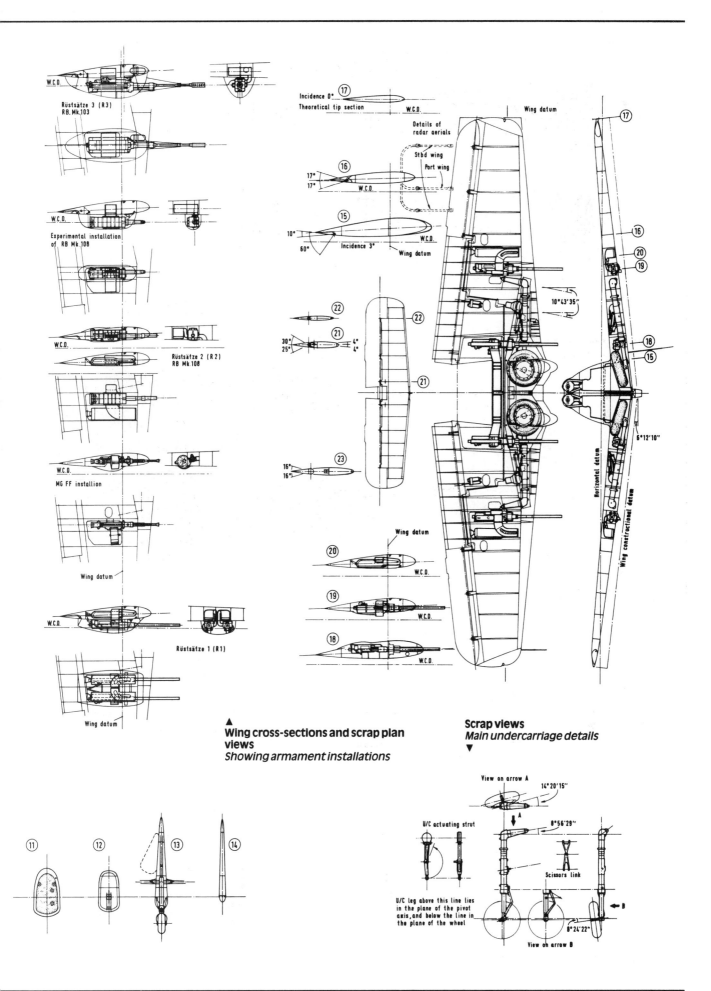

**Wing cross-sections and scrap plan views**
*Showing armament installations*

**Scrap views**
*Main undercarriage details*

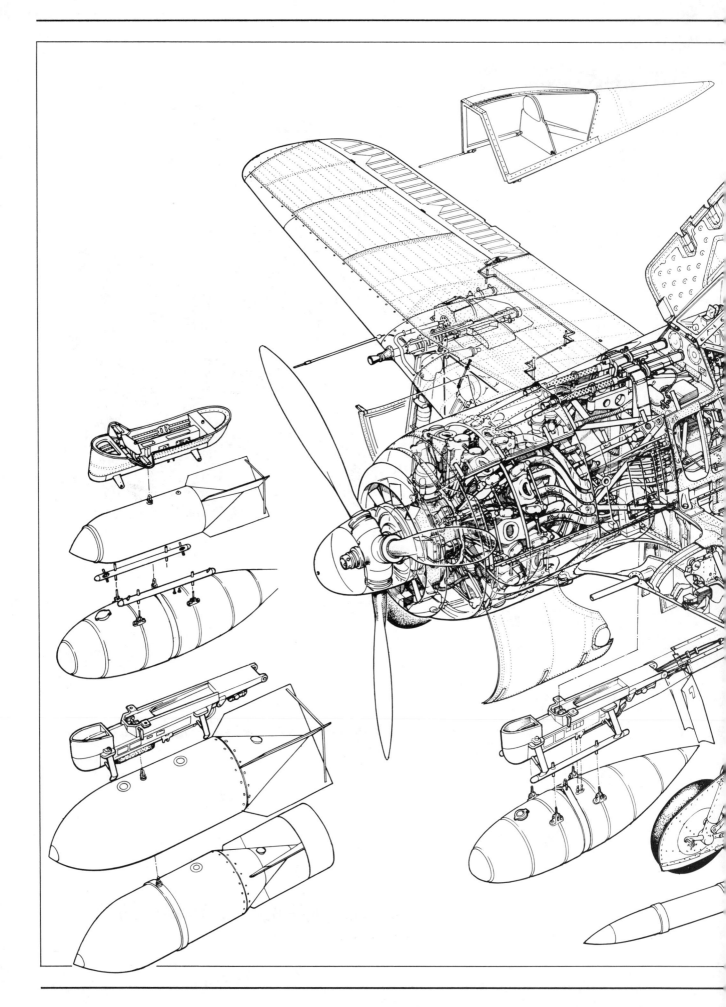

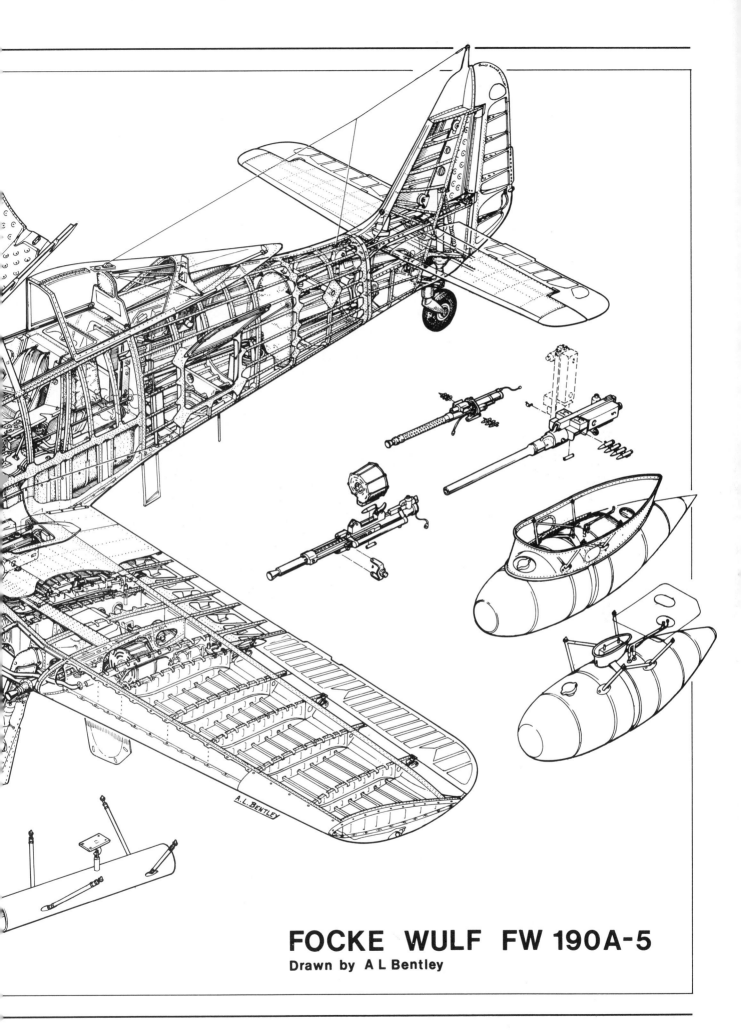

# FOCKE WULF FW 190A-5

**Drawn by A L Bentley**

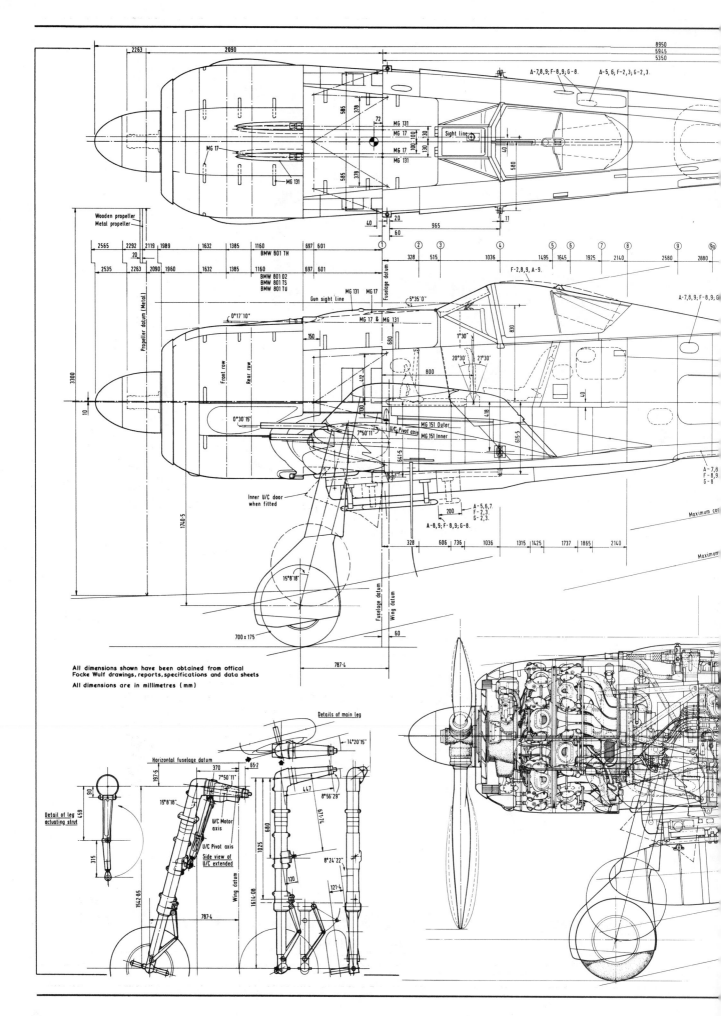

All dimensions shown have been obtained from offical
Focke Wulf drawings, reports, specifications and data sheets

All dimensions are in millimetres (mm)

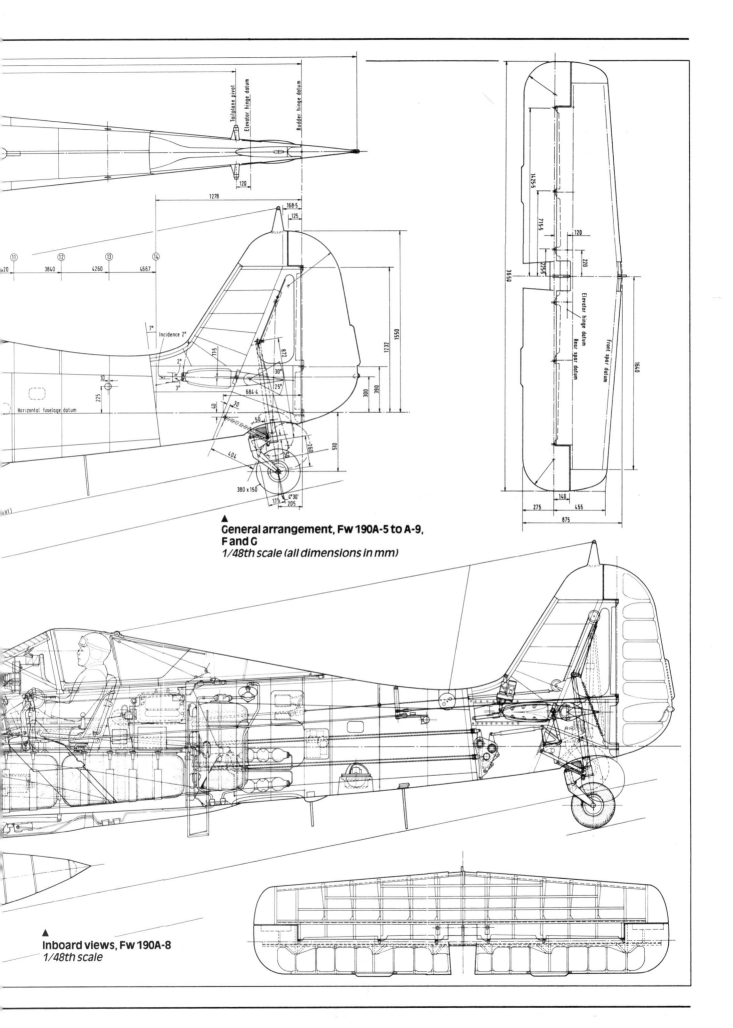

▲
**General arrangement, Fw 190A-5 to A-9, F and G**
*1/48th scale (all dimensions in mm)*

▲
**Inboard views, Fw 190A-8**
*1/48th scale*

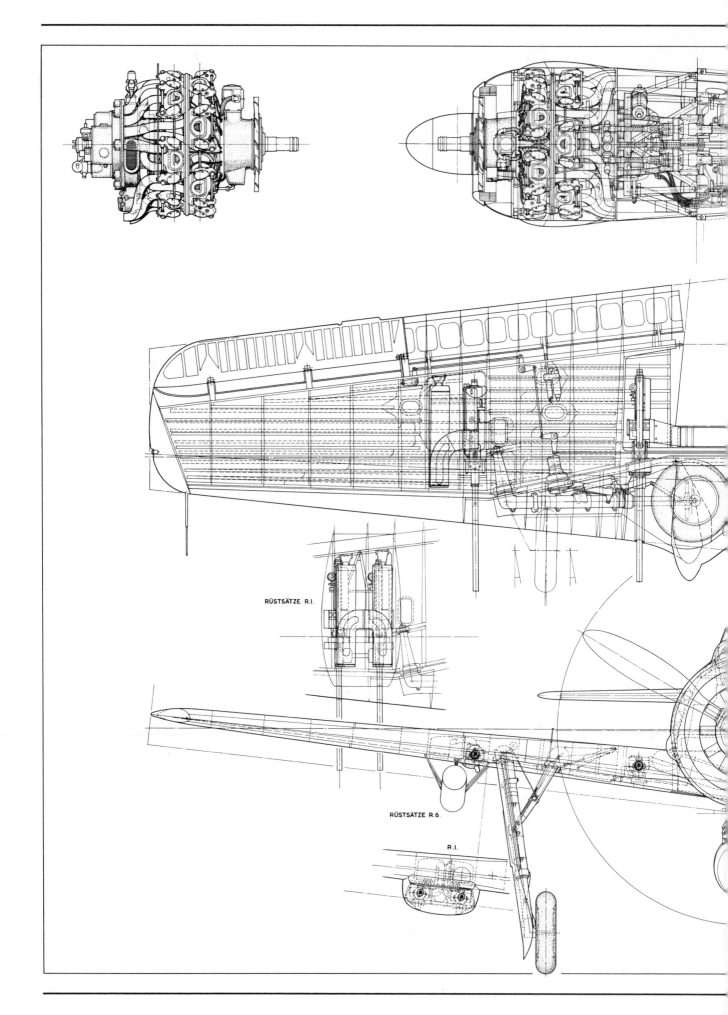

RÜSTSÄTZE R.I.

RÜSTSÄTZE R.6.

R.I.

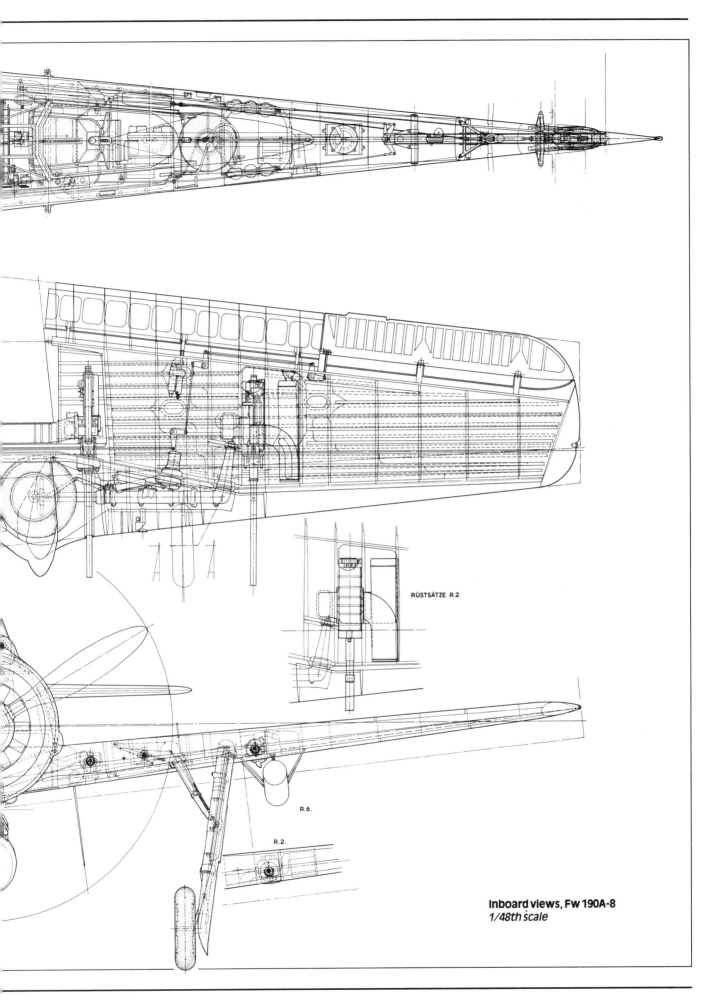

RÜSTSÄTZE R.2.

R.6.

R.2.

**Inboard views, Fw 190A-8**
*1/48th scale*

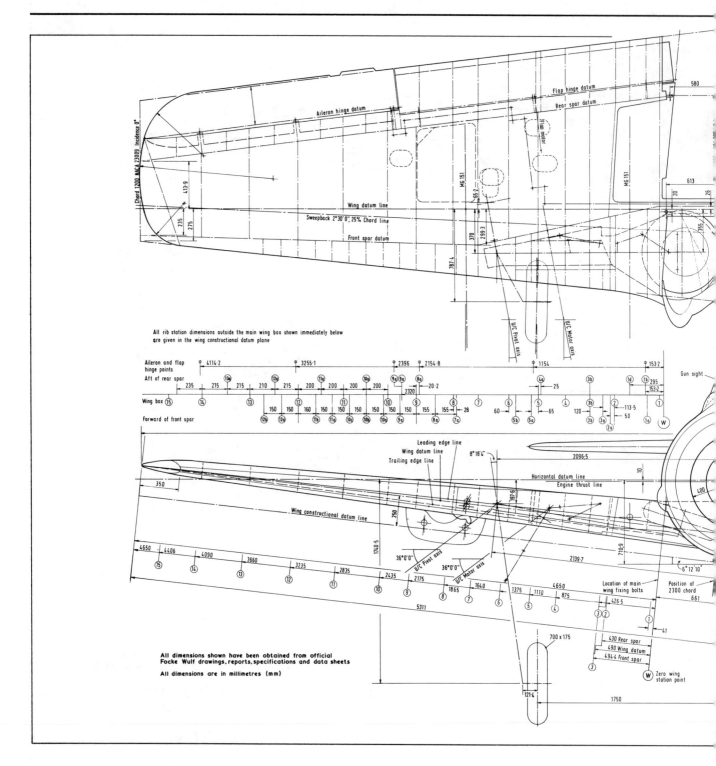

All rib station dimensions outside the main wing box shown immediately below are given in the wing constructional datum plane

Aileron and flap hinge points
Aft of rear spar
Wing box
Forward of front spar

All dimensions shown have been obtained from official Focke Wulf drawings, reports, specifications and data sheets

All dimensions are in millimetres (mm)

Scale

0  1  2  3  4  5  6  7  8 ft
0          1          2 m

**Scrap views ▲ ▶**
*Corrections to night fighter and
two-seat variants (note inboard location
of aerials)*

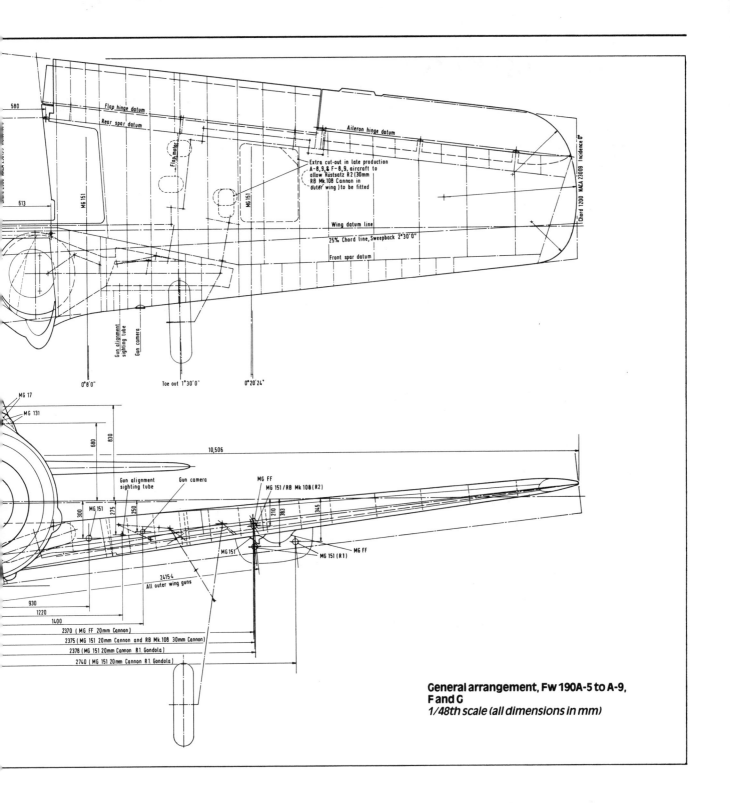

580

Flap hinge datum

Rear spar datum

Flap motor

MG 151

613

MG 151

Aileron hinge datum

Extra cut-out in late production
A-8,9,& F-8,9, aircraft to
allow Rüstsatz R2 (30mm
RB Mk.108 Cannon in
outer wing )to be fitted

Wing datum line

25% Chord line, Sweepback 2°30'0"

Front spar datum

Chord 1200 NACA 23009 Incidence 0°

Gun alignment
sighting tube

Gun camera

0°8'0"

Toe out 1°30'0"

0°20'24"

MG 17

MG 131

680

830

10,506

Gun alignment
sighting tube

Gun camera

MG FF

MG 151 / RB Mk.108 (R2)

300

MG 151

275

250

210

363

345

MG 151

MG 151 (R1)

MG FF

MG FF

2415·4
All outer wing guns

930

1220

1400

2370 ( MG FF 20mm Cannon )

2375 (MG 151 20mm Cannon and RB Mk.108 30mm Cannon)

2378 (MG 151 20mm Cannon R1. Gondola )

2740 ( MG 151 20mm Cannon R1. Gondola )

**General arrangement, Fw 190A-5 to A-9,
F and G**
*1/48th scale (all dimensions in mm)*

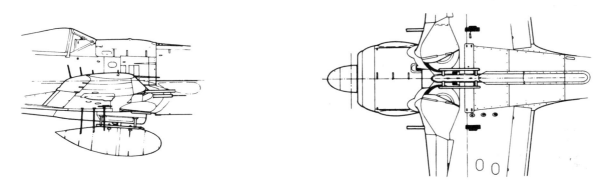

# Martin-Baker MB5

**Country of origin:** Great Britain.
**Type:** Prototype single-seat, land-based interceptor fighter.
**Dimensions:** Wing span 35ft 0in *10.67m*; length 37ft 9in *11.51m*; height 15ft 0in *4.57m*; wing area 262.64 sq ft *24.39m²*.
**Weights:** Empty 9233lb *4189kg*; normal

loaded 11,000lb *4991kg*; maximum 12,090lb *5484kg*.
**Powerplant:** One Rolls-Royce Griffon 83 twelve-cylinder, liquid-cooled piston engine rated at 2340hp.
**Performance:** Maximum speed 460mph *740kph* at 20,000ft *6095m*; initial climb

rate 3800ft/min *1160m/min*; service ceiling 40,000ft *12,190m*; range 1100 miles *1770km*.
**Armament:** Four fixed 20mm Hispano cannon.
**Service:** First flight 23 May 1944.

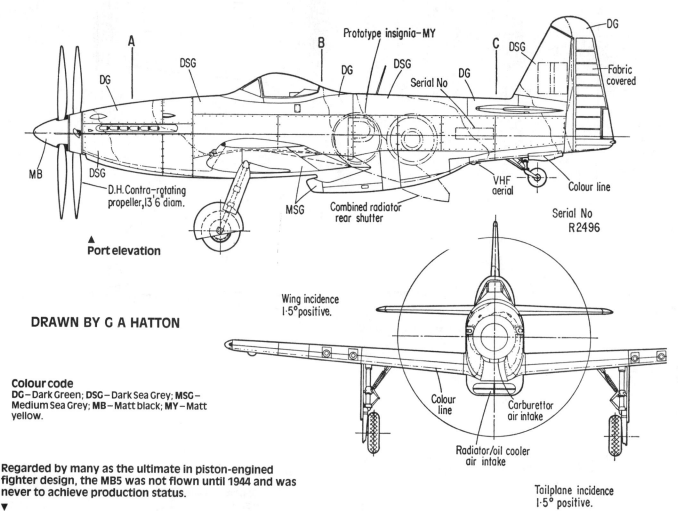

▲ **Port elevation**

**DRAWN BY G A HATTON**

**Colour code**
**DG**–Dark Green; **DSG**–Dark Sea Grey; **MSG**–Medium Sea Grey; **MB**–Matt black; **MY**–Matt yellow.

Regarded by many as the ultimate in piston-engined fighter design, the MB5 was not flown until 1944 and was never to achieve production status.
▼

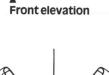

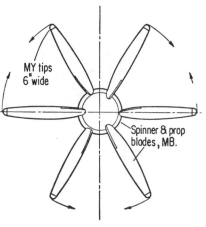

▲ **Front elevation**

▲
The aggressive, purposeful lines of the MB5 are nicely captured in this photo. Note that the camouflage wraps around the wing leading edge.

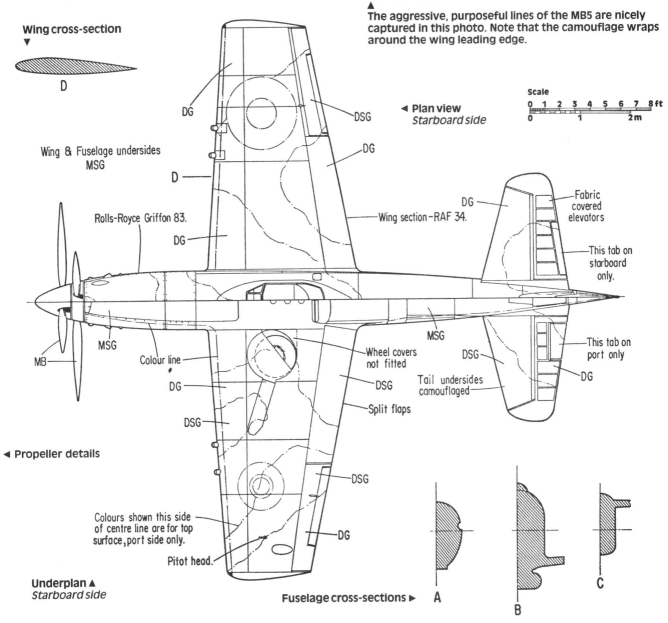

**Wing cross-section**
▼

D

**Wing & Fuselage undersides MSG**

Rolls-Royce Griffon 83.

DG

D

DG

DSG

◄ **Plan view**
*Starboard side*

DG

Wing section–RAF 34.

Scale

0 1 2 3 4 5 6 7 8 ft
0          1          2 m

DG

Fabric covered elevators

This tab on starboard only.

MSG

MSG

Wheel covers not fitted

This tab on port only

MB

MSG

Colour line

DG

DSG

DG

DSG

Split flaps

Tail undersides camouflaged

DSG

DG

◄ **Propeller details**

DSG

Colours shown this side of centre line are for top surface, port side only.

Pitot head.

DG

**Underplan** ▲
*Starboard side*

**Fuselage cross-sections** ►    A    B    C

95

# AIRCRAFT ARCHIVE

## INDEX TO THE SERIES

### FIGHTERS OF WORLD WAR TWO